D0949680

LEADERSHIP SECRETS OF HILLARY CLINTON

REBECCA SHAMBAUGH

New York Chicago San Francisco Lisbon
London Madrid Mexico City
Milan New Delhi San Juan Seoul
Singapore Sydney Toronto

The **McGraw·Hill** Companies

1 2 3 4 5 6 7 8 9 0   DOC/DOC   1 5 4 3 2 1 0

ISBN 978-0-07-166417-2

MHID 0-07-166417-3

McGraw-Hill books are available at special quantity discounts to use as premiums and sales promotions or for use in corporate training programs. To contact a representative, please e-mail us at bulksales@mcgraw-hill.com.

CONTENTS

ACKNOWLEDGMENTS

One of the greatest experiences in writing this book was the opportunity to meet and work with the many extraordinary and knowledgeable people who were invaluable in helping me to weave the chapters, research, and stories together for this book

First, I would like to thank Mary Glenn, my editor from McGraw-Hill, who inspired me to write this book and provided tremendous support throughout the entire process. A special thanks to Tania Loghmani of McGraw-Hill, who helped me to get through many tight deadlines by providing timely and helpful research to support the important messages of this book.

I also want to thank the many accomplished and supportive people who helped me to bring the essence of this book to life. A special thanks to Rebecca Cooper, Dr. Christine Dingivan, Kristin Mannin, Elizabeth Griffith, Reggie Van Lee, Kate Johnson, Candy Crowley, Dee Dee Meyers, and Denise Christy for their knowledge, energy, and openness. And to Lynette Demarest for her extraordinary dedication and expertise in the editing of the book chapters. And to my father, Max Paul Shambaugh, who has been a great role model for resiliency and who encouraged me to realize and tap into my own resilience throughout my journey of leadership and life. Finally, I want to thank the many people in my community and elsewhere across the country and abroad who have heard me speak this past year on this important topic for today's leaders: resilience. They all served as an important source of energy and inspiration not only to write this book but to continue my life's work in developing "great" leaders across this important globe so as to make it a better place for all of us to live.

LEADERSHIP SECRETS OF HILLARY CLINTON

CHAPTER 1

INTRODUCTION

⚜ WHY FOCUS ON LEADERSHIP LESSONS ⚜ FROM HILLARY CLINTON NOW?

Hillary Clinton has always intrigued me—just as she has the rest of the world! Her life, both personal and professional, has been a topic of conversation at dinner tables and water coolers for almost two decades. She has incredibly broad name and face recognition in both the public and private sectors in the United States, Asia, and Europe. Go anywhere in the world and mention her name, and someone will have an opinion of her. While some may agree with her and others disagree, they all recognize her as a global leader who is now in one of the most important leadership roles of her lifetime.

Many people do not understand her formula for leadership success, but most realize that she has one and that she has followed it systematically as she has competed for and won some of the highest leadership positions in our country. They also recognize that her current role as U.S. secretary of state will require that she be an extraordinary leader in these extraordinary times.

Her leadership attributes and skills allow her to be effective in today's turbulent environment, and also to teach others how to be successful as they themselves lead their own organizations and business teams through the global recession that began in 2009. Her leadership lessons are visible and are supported by data as well as by experiential stories that readers will relate to. While many of these "lessons learned" come from her own positive experiences and results, some valuable insights can also be learned from her setbacks.

On a personal note, my experience in speaking at business meetings and conferences in the United States and around the world in the second half of 2009 has highlighted a significant shift in focus—from the theme of general leadership to the specific theme of leadership in turbulent times. And attendees are looking for best practices and solutions that will help them lead through these tenuous times. Both men and women are looking for guidance from those leaders who have successfully navigated through difficult circumstances before and have learned what works and what doesn't work. They appreciate that even great leaders make mistakes, but they value the idea of continuous learning and respect leaders who are able to make midcourse corrections, to move in a different direction, or even to amend a belief that has become an obstacle. They appreciate leaders who can rise above the doom and gloom and succeed in the face of some insurmountable circumstances in a timely way. This is what Hillary Clinton has done for years.

Hillary Clinton's leadership style resonates because it is very different from the leadership approaches that have been successful in the past. She is intellectual, very studied, and a serious thinker. The new business context in which we are operating today requires an innovative approach and a new way of thinking. It needs a leader with the ability to break old patterns of thinking, someone who is willing to take on an unconventional and even risky role in order to be the catalyst for the right change to lead to future success. Hillary's style of leadership studies the facts, articulates a significant view, and demonstrates the ability to build support for specific ideas by "reaching across the aisle." She also has demonstrated the ability to use the right communications style at the right time with the right people in the right way, particularly during difficult and challenging times. Her style ranges from listening intensely and empathizing with others to being diplomatically blunt, and this range has served her well in dealing with the political and relational dynamics involved in all of her roles. Hillary's approach, which she often learned the hard way, has helped her both to achieve her professional goals and to become more widely appreciated over the course of her career.

Whether you have been a follower or even a fan of Hillary's in the past is not the issue for this book. This book is meant to illustrate how someone can come through a long, difficult, and sometimes even weary journey and evolve into one of the most powerful and influential positions in the United States and around the world. You might say that it was pure luck or just hard work. However, based on my 30 years of working with and coaching business leaders, both men and women, I can share with you that, in terms of leadership success, it is not always luck or hard work that gets you there. It is more both an art and a science that good leaders learn and apply to become great. And the good news is that it can be learned by leaders at all levels in an organization if they recognize the key attributes and skills that are most successful in any given circumstances and have a road map for how to learn, adapt, and transform themselves based on the changing environment and the situations at hand.

WHAT LEADERSHIP LESSONS CAN WE LEARN FROM HER?

Hillary has demonstrated the same attributes and skills that I hear being addressed now in businesses around the world, such as being a resilient leader and reinventing your-self and your organization. In order to make it easy for the reader to find and learn from the wealth of experiences that Hillary has had as a leader and to link them to the current conversations that I have with businesspeople every day, I have broken the "lessons learned" into three parts.

First, Hillary provides us with examples of several *unique attributes* that are required of leaders at any level in any organization in the world today, such as being a *continuous learner*, *being resilient*, and *being "adaptively" authentic*.

Second, she provides us with examples of *key leadership skills* that are essential in today's turbulent business environment. These include *being focused*, *being "connected" to people*, and *being a great communicator*.

And, finally, she provides us with a great example of the *heart of a great leader*, which involves *leading with purpose* and *being of service to others*.

In this book, I have tried to capture what resilience is and how one can tap into his own resilience muscle. This is illustrated through stories, personal experiences, and interviews with Hillary Clinton, telling how she found and capitalized on her own resilience. This book will also serve as a practical toolkit that will allow the reader to take her own resilience to the next level. Each chapter has five secrets, which include specific skills, behaviors, and best practices to mobilize greater levels of energy, creativity, communications, relationships, and endurance for dealing with great change, as individuals and within our society, organizations, and intuitions. Each chapter will explore specific areas that will help you home in on how to be the resilient person that you ideally want to be. They are as follows:

- Being resilient
- Being a continuous learner
- Being "adaptively" authentic
- Embracing change
- Being connected
- Being a great communicator
- Having resilience and purpose

CHAPTER 2

OVERCOMING AND THRIVING ON ADVERSITY

Be Resilient

The need for resilient leaders always comes up when I am speaking at conferences, participating in Webcasts, or meeting with executives. At a recent leadership conference, someone asked me what it takes to be a great leader in this turbulent business environment. I shared three things that I believe are essential for being a successful leader today.

1. Leaders need to embrace a positive and proactive attitude toward challenging problems and seize the opportunities that lead to solving them.

2. Leaders need to be comfortable with uncertainty and ambiguity. In fact, they need to be able to make up a new plan as they are implementing the old one!

3. Leaders must be flexible and willing to adapt to change. They are being called upon to reinvent themselves and their organizations over and over again because we haven't gotten to the "new" normal yet.

Then, I went on to explain that these all lead up to one central attribute that I think is most critical for today's leaders, and that is *being resilient*.

It's pretty clear to anyone who is in the job market today that organizations are being forced to steer through many unpredictable and difficult challenges created by both the current economic crisis and the increase in global instability. This calls for a different kind of leader from what was needed in the past, when the focus was on increasing productivity, decreasing costs, and encouraging innovation. Today's leaders must have the ability to weather any kind of storm while effectively making the transitions that are necessary if they are to steer themselves and their organizations through times of great change and uncertainty. These leaders must be resilient because they will not always succeed the first time, and they must be able to garner the same energy and commitment, from themselves and from others, to try again and again until they reach their goals.

Before writing this book, I began to poll my audiences and asked them who they thought was a resilient leader. Over and over again, Hillary Clinton was chosen as the leader who had the most resilient qualities, along with an incredible reserve of energy. Hillary has experienced a life of ups and downs, some of them even tragic from a personal and professional perspective; however, she is best remembered for her ability to bounce back and move forward with even more persistence and sheer determination than any of us could have imagined. That's what makes her so very fascinating to me and what has inspired me to write this book.

This chapter on resilience lays the foundation for the rest of the book by

- Defining resilience
- Explaining its importance in today's business climate
- Introducing you to Hillary Clinton, who is known around the world for her leadership and is recognized for her own resilience throughout the challenging times in her life
- Sharing several of Hillary's secrets for becoming resilient
- Providing tips for assessing your own resilience at this stage in your career

The other chapters of this book address the multiple dimensions of resilience in more detail and provide you with specific tools and techniques to become a resilient leader.

The purist definition of being resilient is having the capacity to recover effectively from misfortunes, disruptive changes, and even failures. We have all experienced disappointments, misfortunes, and failures in our lives. It's part of being human. The question pertaining to your resilience is whether you let these experiences stop you or keep you from pursuing your goals.

Some people say that we are born with this capacity, and others believe that resiliency can be learned. I join the latter school of thought. While I agree that resiliency is driven by an individual's intrinsic qualities, behaviors, and attitudes, and that some of us are more prone to being resilient than others, I also believe that it is possible for all of us to learn how to be resilient and to become a resilient leader. It is even possible for us to teach others.

Hillary Clinton is not a woman who is easily stopped or who throws in the towel very often. Throughout both her personal and her professional life, she has been able to face adversity, adapt to new conditions, and even retool herself in order to get back into the game and come out ahead in most cases.

Rebecca Cooper, a national correspondent for ABC7/WJLA-TV, covered Hillary Clinton during the Clinton administration and shared with me that Hillary's unique combination of intelligence, confidence, and the basic

Midwest values that she grew up with has formed the core of her resilience. Rebecca said, "In Washington, being truly resilient is a difficult commodity to come by, and some people in Washington politics who have experienced great difficulties don't have the strength and inner core to re-emerge as Hillary has been known to do. She is the girl in school whom all of us knew, not just because she was a straight A student but because of her hard work and desire to learn."

This perspective on Hillary Clinton reveals a major aspect of being resilient: staying positive and optimistic even as you face daunting challenges and operating with a sense of purpose and intention through difficult times.

After reading about her and interviewing a number of people who know her well, one thing that is very clear about Hillary is that she is a self-made person. By this I mean that she is responsible for her own success in life and her own sense of resilience through how she has handled her life experiences. She took difficult situations and addressed them as problems to be solved with lessons to be learned. She didn't always get what she wanted, but she also never really failed because she was able to make mid-course corrections and was eventually able to get back on track and be closer to reaching her goals.

Hillary acknowledged this about herself when during one of the Democratic debates, she said, "I think everybody here knows I've lived through some crises and some challenging moments in my life." She elaborated and explained to people that the difficult times in her life enabled her to press forward when the odds appeared to be daunting. Throughout this book, I will share her fascinating stories and the secrets we can learn from her so that you too can tap into your resilience and be recognized for it, both at home and at work.

Helen Keller wisely said, "A happy life consists not in the absence, but in the mastery of hardships." Becoming a great leader begins with your first encounter with misfortune, great desperation, or failure. Each crisis you confront turns into a stepping-stone to greater strength and endurance. Each disruptive change you address gives you greater insight into your leadership abilities. Great leaders are people who look at daunting challenges as opportunities to learn new things and to change in a positive way rather than feeling that they are victims of the situation.

In 1984, the Center for Creative Leadership (CCL) conducted a study on the "key events" that contribute to a leader's development. This study, *Building Resiliency: How to Thrive in Times of Change,* found that the greatest opportunities for leaders to learn, grow, and further their development came during their hardships, lessons learned, failures, and career setbacks. At that time, 34 percent of the respondents indicated that hardships had been their key learning experiences.

Like all of us, Hillary has had her share of hardships, both personal and professional. In her book *Living*

History, she shared a story about how she was always fascinated with exploration and space travel. In fact, at one point, she wrote to NASA and asked how she could become an astronaut. She received a letter back informing her that the agency did not accept girls in the program. She wrote, "It was the first time I had hit an obstacle I couldn't overcome with hard work and determination, and I was outraged. Of course, my poor eyesight and mediocre physical abilities would have disqualified me anyway, regardless of gender. Still, the blanket rejection hurt and made me more sympathetic later to anyone confronted with discrimination of any kind." As a result of this experience, she has been committed to confronting all forms of discrimination and has been a strong supporter of women's rights throughout her career. In fact, she made it clear during her confirmation hearing for secretary of state that women's rights would be a cornerstone of her approach to foreign policy:

Of particular concern to me is the plight of women and girls, who comprise the majority of the world's unhealthy, unschooled, unfed, and unpaid. If half of the world's population remains vulnerable to economic, political, legal, and social marginalization, our hope of advancing democracy and prosperity will remain in serious jeopardy. We still have a long way to go and the United States must remain an unambiguous and unequivocal voice in support of women's rights in every country, every region, on every continent.

Hillary's words and actions resonate resiliency, and your words and actions can, too. Here are five secrets that we can learn from her.

⊹ SECRET 1: UNDERSTAND YOURSELF ⊹

Resiliency is built on self-awareness. This includes knowledge of your values, beliefs, emotions, and attitudes as well as your strengths and weaknesses. It also means recognizing what is holding you back in any given situation. Once you understand this about yourself, you can take a more realistic look at any situation and determine your choices. We always have choices.

For example, if you are asked to make a presentation, but the last time you made one, the feedback was not great, and so you are reluctant to do it again, you can either find a good excuse for not doing it or accept knowing that you will need to figure out how to be more successful this time. Believe it or not, there is no right answer here. It depends on what your goals are, how you can leverage your strengths, and what you think the payoff will be for the amount of effort that it will take you to learn more about making effective presentations. This kind of soul searching will help you see more choices available to you in this particular situation and give you the motivation, courage, and self-confidence to make the choice that is best for you rather than letting the previous bad experience be the deciding factor. This is resiliency: the ability to recognize, in any challenging situation, what is true for you and use this powerful knowledge as your navigation system.

Remember that trying something new can be difficult, and that we can procrastinate and make excuses for not getting out of our own patterns of behaviors and sometimes beliefs about ourselves. Much of that is caused by our own mindset ("I can't do it well" or "doing it takes too much work"), which allows our own voice to talk ourselves out of whatever it is that makes us uncomfortable or frustrated. However, I have found that we create our own obstacles that are based on our own belief system or mindset.

Kate Johnson, senior vice president, service strategy and innovation at Oracle Corporation, uses a sports analogy of someone who has never worked out in his entire life but starts working out at age 40. He feels overwhelmed at the thought of even running around the block. The most important thing to understand is that you don't have to run a marathon the first time. You may have a few stops and starts, but at least you are taking steps to get there. It also helps to break down your overall goal into little bites. Try running for 10 minutes the first time and let yourself build up stamina and endurance. Then run for 20 minutes, and so on, so that you can build your new muscle naturally while building your confidence level as well. When you start seeing incremental levels of progress, you start to shift your mindset from "I can't do" to "I can do."

Kate's example illustrates that many of the obstacles we see are really our own illusions, which can be self-limiting and can ultimately hold us back from being or achieving the things that we really enjoy and could be very good at. It's important to know that we have the power to reexamine and shift our mindsets and reapproach a situation with a more positive and "can do" attitude. When we do this, we are that much more confident and competent, and those obstacles then seem like opportunities. This is an important mindset if we are to be successful in today's environment, as the rules are changing and we are all being asked to or charged with changing our own mindsets from the old way of doing things to a new way of thinking and being.

SECRET 2: CONTROL YOUR IMMEDIATE RESPONSE AND MAKE A PLAN

We all tend to have an immediate reaction to adversity. Some of us avoid the bad news, while others prepare for battle. Knowing your tendency to react one way or the other, and choosing to be proactive rather than reactive, gives you the chance to think about the situation and consider your options before you engage with others about it. This strategy empowers you to stay positive until you have all the information you need to make a judgment about the situation. It also helps you operate with a sense of purpose and intention through the difficult experience. To do this, you have to stay focused on a few key things that resonate with you in terms of what you truly care about. This kind of sustainable focus allows you to *not* get distracted by the adversity, but to use it as a significant source of energy in your life that translates into mapping out and executing a plan.

For example, a friend of mine recently lost her job. When her manager called her into his office to tell her the bad news, her immediate reaction was fear and anger. Why was her team being eliminated instead of another team that wasn't nearly as effective? How would she pay her mortgage if she couldn't find another job? If she had responded immediately, she might have said things that she would later regret. Instead, she asked if she could take a day and then come back and discuss it further with him. She went home, discussed the situation with her family, took some time to figure out her options and what she really wanted for herself, and then prepared to have that next conversation with her boss. As a result, she came away from that conversation with ideas for building and leveraging a broad spectrum of relationships that could help her find a new position and specific ideas for how to make herself more marketable, both inside and outside her company. She learned, based on her conversations with her family and her boss, that she needed to do a better job of quantifying her accomplishments on her résumé. Her boss suggested several people in the company with whom she could do informational interviews to learn more about outside organizations, clients, and partners that she could connect with and explore potential job opportunities.

This is what controlling your response looks like in action.

The second part of this secret is just as important as the first. Putting a plan together gives us back some control of the situation. It moves us in the direction of action, and action begins to shift the circumstances. Action creates energy, and energy promotes resiliency. Whether you pick up the phone and schedule a lunch with someone or decide to go back to school, designing a plan to help you reach your ultimate goals, even if you are starting with baby steps, is moving in the right direction.

⊹ Secret 3: Embrace Change ⊹

The one thing that is constant in life is change. We all know that, but change is still difficult for us. It often presents a threat or involves an uncomfortable adjustment. And resiliency is about overcoming disruptive change—the kind of change that is more difficult than what we normally expect. Having coached many successful leaders, it's clear to me that what differentiates them from ineffective leaders today is their ability to accept and adapt to change. They don't wait for someone to show them what to do. They become their own champions of change.

To do this, you have to understand the human dynamics of change. People strive to maintain the status quo and sustain what is familiar to them. Here's the key to this secret: when you are faced with change, it's time to get curious. *Why, what, how,* and *who* are the questions that you want to be asking. What's the new vision? Who are the key stakeholders? How do they feel about it? Who will benefit and how? And, finally, how can I help implement the change and then ensure that it is sustained?

Embracing change will help you build new skills, broaden your perspective, and enhance your resilience. In the process, you will stand out as a leader and achieve success as a result of the change effort.

My personal experience is that the most difficult changes I have undertaken have created my greatest growth opportunities and have always strengthened both my competence and my confidence. Each change initiative forced me to tap into my creative side, which fostered some of my best planning and provided me with some of my greatest opportunities for visibility as an effective leader. So, I know that this is possible!

When I left my corporate career after 15 years, I wanted to follow up on my burning desire to have my own leadership development company. When I announced that I was leaving the company to start my own organization, I was surprised to get a number of calls from friends and colleagues saying that they were concerned about my well-being and whether I could be successful in running my own organization. While I knew that this was going to be a stretch for me, I also knew that my passion and core strengths were in the leadership development area, and I had always had a burning desire to engage my entrepreneurial spirit. I worked very hard the first year, doing almost everything—from administrative duties to marketing to delivery of the work. I decided that it would also be good for me to get my master's degree in the field of leadership development, so I worked and went to school at the same time. I did focus groups in the local business community and with some of our existing clients to learn from them what was important and a priority in terms of leadership and human capital development and what they would value the most. From there, SHAMBAUGH created an integrated model for developing leaders that still exists today.

I learned through that process that you can do almost anything that you want to do. It starts with a mindset that you believe in yourself, self-accountability. You work hard to learn the ropes, build a supportive network of people around you, and do not waver from your core strengths, value proposition, and brand. Now, 18 years later, SHAMBAUGH is a global leadership and executive development organization that reaches and works with thousands of leaders across the globe.

⊹ SECRET 4: BE COURAGEOUS ⊹

I love the famous quote "The only thing we have to fear is fear itself," because fear is the greatest obstacle to resiliency. Fear causes us to become immobile, ignore our options, and retreat from possibilities. And the best weapon against fear that we have as leaders today is our courage. This courage might mean standing up for what you believe is important, confronting traditional ways of thinking, or even volunteering to do something that you're not sure you can really do. It's usually not something that you can plan for. The need for courage can show up at any time.

Hillary developed her courage early in her life, as both of her parents conditioned her to be strong and confident. In Hillary's autobiography, she talks about how she was reluctant to go outside and play when she was a little girl. She would often come in crying and complaining about Suzy O'Callaghan, a neighborhood girl who was always pushing her around. At age four, when Hillary ran back into the house after another incident with Suzy, her mother told her, "Go back out there, and if Suzy hits you, you have my permission to hit her back. You have to stand up for yourself. There's no room in this house for cowards." Hillary squared her shoulders as she left the house and marched across the street to face Suzy once again. She returned home later glowing with victory and proudly announced, "I can play with the boys now."

Like Hillary, some of us are fortunate enough to have learned about courage at an early age, and others still find it daunting. I advise you to take prudent risks as you leverage your courage at work. If you don't know how to swim, I wouldn't encourage you to ride in a boat without a life vest, but I would encourage you to learn to drive a boat. It's the same principle at work. You want to stretch yourself in lots of situations where you are not totally confident, while still ensuring that you won't crash and burn in the effort.

✠ SECRET 5: NEVER GIVE UP! ✠

We all get discouraged at some point in our lives. We reach a point when we wonder if it wouldn't be easier to just give up. We begin to doubt our own abilities and lose faith in others. The "thrill of victory" is no longer so sweet, and the "agony of defeat" doesn't seem so bad. Our energy is drained, and we've stopped having fun. This is when you need to dig deep inside yourself and find that well of determination and inner strength that will help you face your fears, counter the ensuing complacency, and keep you committed to reaching your goals.

Having this sheer determination is one of Hillary's keys to success. Never being a quitter was wired into her DNA early on and was reinforced while she was still in college. When she first arrived at Wellesley, she struggled academically. She called her parents, hoping that they would tell her to come home. She told them that she didn't feel that she was bright enough or up for the academic challenge. Dorothy Rodham, her mother, told her that she had not raised a quitter and that dropping out of Wellesley would be a catastrophic mistake. Hillary stayed in school and, with her incredible work ethic, keen organizational skills, and sheer determination, stayed on top of her grades. In fact, she gained enough confidence in her scholastic abilities to take on political leadership roles and was elected president of the Young Republicans. Pretty impressive for someone who wanted to drop out of school!

And if you followed the 2008 presidential campaign, you know that Hillary stayed in the race to the very end. She never stopped trying to win votes and secure delegates until it was evident that she was not going to win the nomination. She never gave up on what she was truly committed to doing, even when the odds were against her and the effort to move forward must have been very difficult.

And yet this particular defeat is perhaps the greatest example of her being resilient. While Hillary failed to get the nomination, she showed up at the 2008 Democratic National Convention with a sense of inner confidence and strength and gave an inspirational speech in which she declared her support for the nomination of Barack Obama. She said, "I am here as a proud mother, as a proud Democrat, a proud Senator, a proud American, and a proud supporter of Barack Obama." She followed with, "Whether you voted for me or for Obama, the time is now to unite as a single party with a single purpose." Toward the end of her speech, she shared with the audience that even in the darkest moments, Americans are known for their ability to keep going. She said, "We're Americans, we're not big on quitting. . . . In America, there is no chasm too deep, no ceiling too high, for all who work hard, have faith in God and our country, and each other."

Those words soared through the convention hall, with people rising from their chairs and waving their hands, validating Hillary's words that evening. In some ways, I believe they were acknowledging her ability to come back, be resilient, and gracefully embrace the new reality that she would not be the next Democratic nominee for the president of the United States.

Hillary's words expressed her true intention, which was to serve the country she loved. She even mentioned to some people that she loved her job as a senator and that she could still make a difference by being a senator again, which told everyone that she was not going to just throw in the towel. She knew that her overall desire and purpose was to serve her country, and she made it known that she would do that in whatever capacity the president thought she could do best. Hillary's ability to be flexible and open to other possibilities was instrumental in her not only being resilient but also ending up having the secretary of state role offered to her. Those who can see beyond the horizon and do not stay in the valley and play the victim are those who not only are resilient but also open the door to other possibilities and sometimes great opportunities.

Hillary's resiliency—her unique ability to face adversity and bounce back, as she did in this recent presidential campaign—has won her the respect and admiration of people from all political parties in the United States. And her decision to continue to make a difference by taking on a global leadership role in lieu of being president has impressed people around the world. Truly there are many leadership lessons to be learned from this outstanding woman.

⸙ HOW RESILIENT ARE YOU? ⸙

If you are wondering just how likely you are to be resilient at this point in your life, here are a few easy questions to ask yourself. The more times you answer yes, the more likely you are to tap into your resiliency factor.

1. _____ I'm usually optimistic. I see difficulties as temporary, expect to overcome them, and believe that things will turn out well.
2. _____ I can tolerate high levels of uncertainty and ambiguity.

3. _____ I'm able to recover emotionally from setbacks. I can express my feelings to friends and ask them for help.

4. _____ I feel self-confident and have a healthy concept of who I am.

5. _____ I hold up well during tough times. I have an independent spirit underneath my cooperative way of working with others.

6. _____ I've been made stronger and better by difficult experiences.

7. _____ I've converted misfortune into good luck and found benefits in bad experiences.

8. _____ I demonstrate the courage to stand up for what I believe in or feel is important, and I am not afraid of taking prudent risks.

9. _____ I don't give up easily. I stay the course even when I get discouraged.

10. _____ I am comfortable with change. I look for opportunities to learn new things and visibly support the change efforts.

Consider this initial assessment as a baseline for gauging your resiliency. There may be some areas that you feel good about and other areas that you would like to focus on now. Here are the five secrets again.

SECRETS FOR RESILIENCY

Secret 1: Understand yourself.

Secret 2: Control your immediate response and make a plan.

Secret 3: Embrace change.

Secret 4: Be courageous.

Secret 5: Never give up!

CHAPTER 3

SMART POWER

Be a Continuous Learner

One hallmark of great leaders is their capacity to learn continuously throughout their lives. You've probably heard the quote: "If you have never failed, you have never learned, and you cannot lead." While formal education is very important, I'm talking about the kind of learning that becomes your life journey. It involves being curious and wanting to learn more about something—a compulsion to know as much or even more about a subject than others do—and learning from both your successes and your failures. It takes courage because you have to be able to face new and challenging situations and often operate in unfortunate circumstances. These experiences give you critical learning opportunities—your chances to objectively ask yourself the hard questions: *What did I do well? What could I have done differently? What can I learn from this?* This is what I mean by *continuous learning*.

When I speak on the topic of leadership at conferences around the world, I always say that leadership is really about listening, *learning*, and then leading. And it is essential for today's leaders to do this because of the fast pace and constant change that are inherent in the business world. As we as leaders face new challenges, we must be able to draw on our knowledge and experience, apply these insights to new situations, and then decide wisely.

Hillary Clinton is a continuous learner. One of her long-standing and great strengths has always been her desire to learn. As a little girl, she loved working her way through the books in the children's section of the library. Today, as a public figure, her supporters describe her as being well read while her critics refer to her as a "policy wonk" or an intellectual nerd. But they all agree on one thing: Hillary does come up to speed fast on any topic that she's going to discuss or any project that she is going to take on. And she always has done so. Whether it was learning how to play a board game as a child, improving her math skills as a student, or preparing to debate her father on an issue at the dinner table, she was determined to immerse herself in that area in order to build both her competence and her confidence.

Throughout her career, she has continued to take on new roles and work on issues that stretched her knowledge base and expanded her skill sets. She rose from being a lawyer in Arkansas to U.S. senator from New York to being one of the most powerful women in the world as U.S. secretary of state. Her innate curiosity and her desire to learn enabled her to transform her career. In each role, she stepped out of her comfort zone, worked hard to learn the ropes, and prepared herself for the challenging opportunity.

One example of Hillary's stepping out of her comfort zone was when she took a leap of faith and decided to run for the Senate. When she was considering running, she sought advice from her colleagues and close friends to see whether they thought it was a good idea. While she received encouragement from some, other close friends discouraged her from running, saying that life on the campaign trail would be grueling; she would be living on a airplane and running a marathon from one part of the state to another. Hillary herself also had doubts about whether Congress was where she could have the greatest impact and be most effective. She also was anxious about the fact that she would really be on her own and not aligned with Bill Clinton, which had never been the case before.

There were many reasons for her not to run for the Senate, but then she had an awakening moment. She attended an event in New York City promoting an HBO special about women in sports. She was accompanied by Billie

Jean King, a longtime tennis legend. They were joined by many young women athletes, who were assembled on the stage with a large banner behind them that said, "Dare to Compete," the title of the HBO film. Then the captain of the girls' basketball team at the high school where the event was being held, Sofia Totti, introduced Hillary. Hillary went to shake her hand, and Sofia leaned forward and whispered in her ear, "Dare to compete, Ms. Clinton." "Dare to compete." This caught Hillary so much off guard that it got her thinking after she left the event. In her own words, as shared in *Living History*, she thought, "Could I be afraid to do something I had urged countless other women to do?" She then said, "Why am I vacillating about taking on this race? Why aren't I thinking more seriously about it? Maybe I should 'dare to compete.'"

This encouragement from Sofia was an important turning point for Hillary to move beyond her comfort zone. Hillary's inner beliefs, values, and inner strengths began to take over her thought process, and she knew that running for the U.S. Senate would be hard and challenging, but if it wasn't hard, then everyone would do it—being hard was what made it important and great. Smart leaders approach a challenge with a positive yet realistic mindset. They move beyond the assumptions or beliefs of others and find their core strengths, beliefs, and intentions, all of which serve as the compass and give them the confidence to tackle almost any challenge.

Hillary's spiritual side also came out when she reached out for advice and received a boost from George Tribou, the priest who for many years had run the Catholic boys' high school in Little Rock, whom the Clintons had become friends with during the past years. Father Tribou wrote a letter to Hillary dated June 24, 1999, which stated his view in these words: "On Judgment Day the first question God asks is not about the Ten Commandments . . . , but what He asks each of us is this: 'What did you do with the time and the talents I gave you?'" This helped Hillary to look inward to remind herself of her many years of campaigning, which had turned into a core strength of hers. She then tapped into another innate strength, which was to organize a diverse spectrum of people around her to help her achieve her goals and deal with the challenges ahead of her. She set up committees to better assess the challenges that she had in front of her and the best strategy for addressing them. She also knew that she couldn't just talk to the people of New York, but needed to work hard to get out there, listen to and learn from the people of New York, and demonstrate that what she was for was more important then where she was from.

She never felt intimidated by the situation, but she always felt that it was important for her to roll up her sleeves, take the time to learn everything that she needed to know, reflect on her performance, and learn from her mistakes to ensure even greater success the next time.

When you are moving beyond your comfort zone, be smart and assess your gaps or challenges. Then make a prudent plan to address them. Great leaders also identify and tap into their core strengths when they are walking into any new or challenging situation. This reinforces a sense of inner confidence as they walk into the unknown. Finally, prepare to work hard, to study up, and to listen and learn. Just having this attitude will show other people that your intentions are good, and they will be more willing to support you along the way. This one example illustrates that Hillary is a master at *continuous learning,* and you can be one, too. Here are five secrets to help you get started.

✴ SECRET 1: CONTINUE TO BUILD ✴ YOUR SELF-AWARENESS

Experience tells us that what makes a great leader is the capacity to look inward and gain a clear and truthful sense of your values, your biases, your intentions, your strengths, and your weaknesses. In my previous book, *It's Not a Glass Ceiling, It's a Sticky Floor,* I discussed seven self-limiting beliefs, assumptions, and behaviors that hold women back from achieving their career goals. A key to addressing these personal obstacles is recognition of what they are as they play out in your own life. This is called *self-awareness.* It requires introspection about the core of who you are—the vision you have for your life, those few things that are ultimately most important to you, and how you define "success" for yourself.

As a business leader, you also need to understand yourself in relation to your leadership effectiveness. In two decades of research at SHAMBAUGH Leadership, we've found that the areas that will have a significant impact on your ultimate success include power and influence, business savvy, team building, encouraging innovation, managing change, building strategic relationships, strategic thinking, managing upward, and effective collaboration. For these areas, as well as others that are important to you, you need to be getting ongoing feedback regarding both your performance and your reputation. How are you doing? What results are you getting? What are your strengths and weaknesses? What are your blind spots? How are you providing value? How are you being perceived by others in your organization?

While many organizations today are using 360-degree leadership feedback instruments to help leaders gain these insights, increasing your self-awareness also requires more timely feedback. You need several individuals whom you both respect and trust to give you ongoing situational feedback on a regular basis. This feedback is what keeps your self-awareness learning alive and relevant.

⊹ SECRET 2: GET OUT OF ⊹
YOUR COMFORT ZONE

Have you ever heard the term *prudent risk*? I remember learning long ago about "blue rules" and "red rules"—blue rules are things that you know you can or should do, and red rules are things that you know you can't or shouldn't do. When I was a kid, a red rule in a hospital used to be that no one could smoke around an oxygen tank—never (because it could blow up). There were no exceptions to this rule. That was a red rule. But a nurse could decide that a patient shouldn't be awakened at 7 a.m. for breakfast if he had not slept well that night. And she could make this decision any time, at her discretion. That was a blue rule. But what about the *purple* zone? Those are the choices that in business we call "challenges" and "opportunities"—situations where we don't have the security of clear guidelines or reasonable expectations to fall back on when making decisions. I call these "prudent risks," and because we don't know the outcome, they take us out of our comfort zone.

When I'm talking or coaching leaders about this, I often ask them to think about a time in their lives when they learned one of their greatest lessons or had one of their greatest breakthroughs. Then I ask them to describe those situations, and just about every story I hear involves an experience in which they took a prudent risk. Some of these situations have happy endings and some don't. It doesn't seem to matter. Our personal and professional growth can come from either one because it's not the outcome of the experience that has the greatest impact on us; it's the journey and what we learn along the way.

Scary? Yes, taking risks can be scary. And it is always hard work. But I've found that it is easier to make those risky choices if you make them because you are truly committed to something, whether your choices stem from a passion that you have for yourself or a vision that you have for others around you. For example, I've always been driven to stay on top of the learning curve in everything that I do and care about. I'm actually pretty passionate about it. I remember that when I worked in corporate America (for close to 15 years), I often took on new jobs that I was totally unqualified for—those that were a real stretch for me—just to see the business from a whole new perspective.

I got a call one evening from a man named Bob, who was the corporate human resource officer at Fairchild Industries, which was located on the East Coast. He had heard about me from his network and said that he was looking for someone to take on the human resources leadership role at Fairchild's corporate headquarters. I was living in the Midwest and in fact was happy in my current job, working as director of human resources for a company that had a major division in Indianapolis, Indiana. I loved living in Indianapolis, all my close friends and family were nearby, and I certainly was not looking for a change in my existing role. Yet, after a two-hour phone conversation, Bob convinced me to at least come to the firm's headquarters in the greater Washington, D.C., area and interview for the job. So I said to myself, "What do I have to lose?" Once I learned more about the job, I realized that this role was a bit over my head, as it involved taking the lead on some major human resource initiatives; in one way this would be exciting, yet nothing I had ever done had had the scope and responsibility that this job would entail. Then, at the same time, another company in Chicago, Standard Oil (as it was at the time), was trying to recruit me to take a job at its headquarters heading up one aspect of its recruiting. I had done recruiting before and was very confident in that competency area. And I loved Chicago and thought that it would be a fun city to live in.

Over the course of several weeks, I went back and forth, now with two job offers, from Fairchild and from Standard Oil of Indiana, to consider. I had three choices: stay in my existing role in Indianapolis or take one of the other two jobs. The Midwest was near and dear to me, and I had strong family ties and friendships there. Yet I realized that while it was nice and comfortable, I had never really had that "stretch" job, one in which I would immerse myself in something new, learn, grow, and broaden my own business and leadership perspective and muscle. After many conversations with my friends and family and with myself, I had an awakening moment, realizing that sometimes staying in our comfort zone can be good for important reasons in our personal life, yet it can also be self-limiting. I was still young, 32 years of age, and I asked myself, "What is the worst that can happen if I take the job in the East Coast?" There were certainly pluses in taking a job that would provide a rich and deep level of experience that in the short run and the long run would provide a higher level of compensation and, more important, would be a great stepping-stone that would set me up for many other choices and opportunities in my career. It also would give me the chance to live in an entirely different part of the United States, which, since I was a girl from the Midwest, would expand my own experience of what it's like to live in a new and exciting place in our country—the backyard of the White House.

I then said to myself, "What's the greatest fear that I have about whether I can manage that?" A big fear was just the unknown and not being able to fulfill the expectations of the job. Yet I knew myself, and I have always been a good learner who was willing to immerse myself in the new job while finding some good mentors who would support me along the way. I then said, "I will give myself two years, and if the new job doesn't work out, I will come back to the Midwest and rebuild my career and life there again." I ended up taking the job and staying at Fairchild for six years. It was an opportunity of a lifetime for me, and it opened up many new doors for me from a learning and relationship perspective. It also tapped into and strengthened my resilience muscle, as I was trying something that was outside my own comfort zone, something that involved stepping into the unknown, experiencing change, and hard work. This experience made me stronger, wiser, and more confident to accept the new opportunities and roles that I have taken on in my life.

Sometimes, our own voice will talk us out of taking the kinds of risks that can build not only our competence but also our sense of confidence and resilience. While I took prudent risks along the way, each new experience reinforced my confidence in taking on new assignments, learning the ropes, and acquiring a set of skills that were unique to that job. This desire to stretch and continuously learn strengthened my business acumen, enhanced my résumé, and eventually led me to start my own company.

One of Hillary's most difficult decisions was deciding whether she should run for the Senate. While she had campaigned for her husband, this was a whole new ball game, in which she would be required to campaign for herself. She knew that she not only had to raise $25 million to run the campaign but also would need to physically cover 54,000 square miles to gain votes throughout the state. This meant that she would be spending her time meeting and talking with people who represented a diverse spectrum of social views, economic circumstances, and cultures, and who would often have competing political agendas. From the

White House to representing New York State. Talk about getting out of your comfort zone! And she certainly did.

While the challenges and opportunities that come your way may seem as daunting to you as this did to Hillary, try "stretching" with small things at first—volunteer to do something that you've never done before or agree to talk with someone who you'd never imagine would want to talk with you. I remember coaching a bright, intelligent, and accomplished woman who had made her mark in medicine as a successful surgeon. She later took a job in industry in the biosciences area. Her intellectual horsepower and scientific knowledge were important factors in her ability to bring immediate value to her new job and the organization. However, the executives of the organization saw potential in her, and she was advanced to a leadership position. She liked the many aspects of leading others and enjoyed tapping into this unrealized strength of hers that was significantly different from being a surgeon in many ways.

We both worked together as she mapped a future career track. She decided that she wanted to set a goal of being a chief medical officer within her existing organization or at another company. To do this, she needed a broader and stronger level of financial acumen. I asked her to think about her own relationships and identify who might be able to help her or be a resource of knowledge for her. She ended up reaching out to the CFO of her organization and asking if he would be interested in meeting with her for the next several months and together engaging in cross-mentoring each other—the CFO would inform and broaden her acumen on the financial side, while she, in turn, would share her medical and scientific knowledge. This ended up being a win-win for both. They ended up enjoying the relationship and became good friends over time.

Whether it's reaching out and asking for advice, mentoring for someone you know, or even volunteering to serve at a hospital if you are concerned about the care and nurturing of others, have some fun with it. And with each experience that takes you out of your comfort zone, be sure to ask yourself: What did I learn from this? What did I do well, and what would I do differently? Finally, don't be discouraged if you make a few mistakes. That comes with the territory.

⸸ SECRET 3: DO YOUR HOMEWORK ⸸

I like to bring this up in discussions about continuous learning because it usually brings back memories for all of us. Whether you were one of those students who got right to it or one who finished at the last minute, few of us doubted the *benefits* of completing our homework when it came time for those exams. Being prepared not only gets you better results, but helps you build your confidence.

When Hillary was running for the Senate seat, she increased her chances for success by doing her homework.

She knew that she needed to prove to New York voters that she understood the issues that their families faced and prove her determination to work for them. While she could have had her staff prepare briefings for her about this, she knew that it would be better if she saw and heard for herself what life was like for people on Main Street. She orchestrated a series of "listening tours" that allowed her to hear firsthand from New York citizens about their hopes, fears, issues, and concerns. She covered 62 counties, traveling from one local spot to another in a converted Ford van, which the press nicknamed the HRC Speedwagon. She visited coffee shops, diners, and town halls. She went into people's homes and spoke with groups sitting around a dining room table. As a result of her effort, people began to see Hillary as someone who was genuinely interested in them, and they began to feel comfortable sharing their concerns and stories with her. She learned the right questions to ask, and she gathered her answers in the form of mental images and personal stories. By the time she was done, not only did she have all the answers for the exam, but she could write the exam herself!

One of the chapters in my *Sticky Floors* book is about leveraging your political savvy. Tina Sung, vice president of government transformation for Partnership for Public Service, often talks to women in our SHAMBAUGH Leadership programs about the positive aspects of being politically savvy, and she links doing your homework in business to this critical leadership competency. The more you understand something, the better you can figure out how to deal with it. This means learning not only everything you can about a topic but also about particular situations. For example, Tina encourages women to ask questions like

- What's the context?
- What are the facts and assumptions?
- Who are the key players, and what are their positions?
- Who has the power and is making the decisions?
- Who is affected, and what is their reaction?
- Where can I provide value?
- What results or outcomes do I want?
- What's the process for getting there?
- What are the potential consequences?
- What could go wrong?
- What is my exit strategy?

Doing your homework is a critical part of continuous learning. And once you become recognized as someone who does it consistently and does it well, not only will you have more confidence but others will also have more confidence in you.

⚜ SECRET 4: LEARN FROM YOUR MISTAKES ⚜

During the Clinton White House days, both Hillary and Bill were perceived as being bad listeners. They often forged ahead and worked from their own set of beliefs and operating principles. One of Hillary's greatest leadership lessons came when she established the President's Task Force on National Health Care Reform. Her passion for this topic had started back in Arkansas, where she had taken a significant role in improving health care for young children. Although she applied her prior knowledge and experience to this massive undertaking, it got off to a poor start. She felt passionately that the health-care policy that she and her committee were proposing was the most efficient and effective one out there, and in some cases those who criticized her plan were blocked out so that their voices were not heard. She even had her own "war room," primarily staffed by members of her political party who shared her views, and she directed her team to block any "attacks" on her health plan. Donna Shalala, who was on the Council of Economic Advisors at the time, warned Hillary that she needed to build a broad base of support across party lines if she was to be successful, but, for many reasons, that never happened, and this effort became one of Hillary's greatest regrets. But from this experience, she learned that no matter how passionate or right you feel about something, you need to listen to the views of others if you want them to listen to you. This has already been illustrated in detail on her listening tour in New York and her shift to being more collaborative and inclusive when she was in the Senate.

And, if we are truly engaged in continuous learning, the one thing that is certain is that we'll make mistakes. The only fatal mistake is one that you don't learn from. In many organizations, projects are reviewed periodically in terms of "lessons learned," with the focus being on improvement rather than on blame. I think that this is the mindset we all need to have when we know that we tried our best but things just didn't turn out the way we wanted them to.

✢ SECRET 5: LEARN FROM OTHERS ✢

I have always been a curious person. As a little girl growing up in the Midwest, I was always asking "why" or "how" questions because I didn't want to miss out on anything that was happening around me. My father had a huge influence on me. Watching him build one of the largest general contracting firms in the country was one of my greatest learning experiences. The construction industry was and still is a very tough and competitive business. To be successful, it is critical to stay informed and connected to both the customers and the employees. My father didn't wait for the information that he needed to come to him;

rather, he was constantly out in the field, speaking with employees, customers, and community leaders to understand the major concerns, problems, and opportunities in their day-to-day work and to determine the latest trends in the marketplace. He then used this information to make adjustments in terms of how he ran the company and how SHAMBAUGH & Son could reinvent itself to become and remain a leader in the building industry. I learned from my father's example that you can't wait for someone to give you the instruction booklet. You have to take the initiative, roll up your sleeves, be open to listening, and constantly look at ways to stay on top of your game while you are consistently bringing value to others. In many ways, my father has been my lifelong mentor.

And I've had many other mentors along the way. Some I've learned simply by observing them in action, others have been sources of information and insight, and many have given me feedback that has been invaluable. Some have been older than I, like my father, and some have been younger, like the 23-year-old who taught me all about social networking. Some have been employees in my organization, and others have been customers or even competitors. The one thing they all had in common is that they all had something to teach me.

And finally, if you don't already have your own personal "board of directors," now is a good time to begin recruiting one. The people on it are individuals whom you trust and respect and who care enough about you and your success that they will answer your questions, give you their wise advice, and connect you with others who can be a further resource to you. They are a special type of mentor because they usually know you very well and stay with you over an extended period of time. They not only help you with specific situations in the short term but also help you establish longer-term strategies for your career and your life.

✛ How Much of a Continuous ✛
Learner Are You?

Here are a few questions to see where you might be on the spectrum of continuous learning:

1. Are you clueless about how other people perceive you? If you do know what others think of you, is it the same as the way you perceive yourself?
2. Do you feel as though you have lost your creative spark? Are you bored with your everyday routine?
3. Do you feel burned out or less motivated in your current job than you have in other roles that you've had in the past three years?
4. Are you constantly looking at ways to bring a new and different value to your current job?
5. Have you had an idea that you have always dreamed about pursuing but haven't done as yet?

6. Have you received direct feedback (on your leadership in general or on a specific skill) that says that you need further development?

7. Do you want to be considered for that next level of responsibility or for an area in which you have a strong interest, but you are not totally competent to fill that role?

8. Do you hesitate before taking on a new "stretch" project for fear of failure?

9. Can you name at least 10 people who have helped you grow and develop over the past year?

10. Are you soliciting feedback, support, and advice from others on a regular basis?

If you are not happy with your answers to any of these questions, you might want to focus on your continuous learning. Here are the five secrets again.

SECRETS FOR CONTINUOUS LEARNING

Secret 1: Continue to build your self-awareness.

Secret 2: Get out of your comfort zone.

Secret 3: Do your homework.

Secret 4: Learn from your mistakes.

Secret 5: Learn from others.

CHAPTER 4

AUTHENTICITY

The Core of Resilience

Leadership is not what we do, but rather who we are. The foundation of who we are is our authentic self-expression of our values—what we stand for and how we measure up to others. It's the basis of the conversations that people have about us when we leave the room.

It's a given that you need to have both substance and business acumen to lead in today's business environment; however, what keeps leaders centered, focused, and able to make tough decisions is their authenticity. Put simply, authenticity is acting in alignment with your values and core beliefs. Your values are those things that you believe represent right and wrong as well as what you believe defines success for you and others. Authenticity involves knowing what's really important to you, what you are committed to, and what your priorities are in both the short and the long term. This gives you a true sense of direction along with a clear purpose and vision for yourself. It serves as a compass in your life that promotes consistency in what you say and do. When others see this consistency, they are more likely to trust you, respect you, and be willing to follow you.

This aspect of leadership is critical in today's climate because it provides an anchor for leaders who are dealing with so much change and uncertainty while constantly facing new challenges. It also serves as a timely navigation system to let leaders know when they are getting off the track and need to make midcourse corrections if they are to be successful. It gives them confidence to ride out the storm and not be influenced by false notions or minor setbacks.

However, I want to point out that you can't instantly become authentic—rather, it takes a series of life experiences and a commitment to learn from those experiences to shape your true authentic self.

⊹ HILLARY'S AUTHENTICITY ⊹

Hillary Clinton is one of the most fascinating women in politics today. She has been in the public eye for almost two decades, and yet many political analysts keep asking, *Who is*

Hillary Clinton? I am not sure that there is a simple answer to that question, but her career over the past few years has certainly given us a better opportunity to see that along with her tremendous intellect and drive for results, she has some very endearing personal characteristics.

On the presidential campaign trail, she emphasized her experience relative to that of her opponents, which in some ways put her out there as a "celebrity." When you are in that situation, people tend to put you under a microscope and report on or talk about everything that you do and say. However, by then there was already a significant shift in how people perceived the "real" Hillary from the past view, which was less compassionate, passionate, and internally driven.

Things started to change when she began to campaign for and won the New York Senate seat. During the campaign, she was repeatedly seen as curious, caring, and concerned. In 2006, Dan Ackman with Elaine S. Povich wrote in "President Hillary Clinton?" published on Forbes.com, "She appears to be thinking through each answer to a question, even if she's heard it many times before. She makes eye contact and sprinkles her comments with touches of wit. She knows she's on the record, yet there's the feeling that her answers in private would be much the same."

Hillary became known for actually listening to what the people of the state of New York were telling her as she visited each small town. And when she won that senatorial election, her behavior in the Senate surprised a number of her Senate colleagues, who thought that she would be more opinionated and calculating and very demanding. On the contrary, Hillary did not expect any preferential treatment and did not seek the limelight. Instead, she demonstrated her hard work ethic and her desire to build consensus through meaningful relationships. In an article for the *New York Times,* writer Adam Nagourney described Hillary as "the celebrity senator who is forever offering to bring a colleague a cup of coffee, or volunteering to sit in as a presiding officer in the deserted chamber on a Friday night, or stepping back at news conferences to let other senators speak." In *A Woman in Charge,* author Carl Bernstein commented, "She worked particularly hard for those who didn't support her, as if to prove to them that she wasn't who they thought she was." She became recognized as a strong listener as well as an experienced debater—who also had a keen sense of humor. This was the beginning of a very important turning point for Hillary, as she began to show more of her "true" or authentic self. She was successfully standing on her own as both a candidate and a senator. And she was doing it her way.

When she was campaigning for senator from New York, Hillary didn't think that giving speeches would explain the private part of who she was. So she attended small and intimate gatherings at people's homes in many areas of the state.

Hillary shared in her book *Living History* that she would talk to people more informally and answer their questions about her marriage, why she moved to New York, health care, child care, and whatever else was on their minds.

What people began to recognize and appreciate was Hillary's natural warmth and true concern for others. Her strong drive and ambition were still evident, yet the endearing aspects that were being talked about were more on a personal level, such as her unselfish ability to praise others and remember meaningful details about their lives.

When people began to see Hillary as the whole person that she was, they responded positively to her because people generally like and support someone who feels comfortable in her own skin and is confident enough to show her more personal or "human" side. This positive response enabled Hillary to become even more confident in and accepting of her true self, which she began to reveal more as time went on. She then headed into the presidential campaign, where she won nearly 18 million fans and earned a place in history for receiving more votes for a nominee in a major political campaign than any other woman in history.

⟶ YOUR AUTHENTICITY STARTS WITH YOU! ⟵

Hillary has found success by showing her authenticity as a leader. So, why can't we understand the power that authenticity has, within ourselves and others, earlier in our careers? Some people need to figure out who they are their own, and some reach out for coaching or mentoring. The bottom line is that the sooner you can understand the core of who you are as a leader and intentionally show yourself that way, the more successful you will be. Whether you already know and live as an authentic leader or you are in the process of defining your authenticity, this chapter will give you some practical ways to build upon or develop this important aspect of your leadership.

⊹ SECRET 1: ACCEPT WHO ⊹ YOU ARE AS A LEADER

Remember that your internal compass and authentic self start with who you are inside, not how others see you or want you to be. Once you start being more your true self, you will experience a stronger sense of validation and internal confidence. This starts with establishing a comfort level with who you really are as a leader. It's important for you to take the time to step back and identify your core leadership values and principles. Then you need to "walk the talk."

Take a moment to ask yourself why people follow you as a leader. Is it because of what you do or because of who you are? Most likely, it's more about who you are than about what you do. To be authentic, you need a deep sense of self-knowledge. Then you have to be willing to accept yourself and reflect your values in your decisions and actions. And once you identify those critical aspects of who you are, it's important that you leave time for self-reflection, for asking yourself not only how you are doing but also if you are doing the right things.

The following set of questions will help you start shaping or reshaping your authentic self as a leader:

Leadership values: what's most important to you?
- What are your top five leadership values, and how would you prioritize them in your role today?
- How have you handled situations in which these values were in conflict with your actions?
- To what extent do you deviate from your leadership values when you are under pressure?

Leadership principles: what are your core beliefs?
- What are the principles that guide your leadership behavior and actions? Do you share those principles with others?
- If you disregarded one of your top leadership principles, what would the loss or consequence be for you? How would getting off course affect your credibility and the respect that others have for you?
- Do your leadership principles align with your current role as a leader?

I remember attending a dinner with Hillary in George-town right around the time she announced her candidacy for the Democratic nomination for U.S. president. As we spoke in small groups, a prominent business leader asked Hillary why she wanted to run for the presidency after all the badg-ering she had received from the press. He asked, "Do you really want to go through this again?" Hillary answered, "There is nothing more to dig up about me. I have been beat up as much as anyone. I am less about changing people's minds now and more interested in being myself."

Having a deeper knowledge of who you are and what's important to you as a leader is only half of being authentic. The other critical half is accepting who you are. You have to recognize and accept your flaws along with your strengths. One prime example is when Hillary was first lady and was leading the health-care reform initiative. While she was dedicated to improving health care for all Americans, she later learned and admitted that how she went about it created conflict in perceptions of her own intentions and leadership, She learned that taking a more 360-degree view of the world rather than working and leading in a vacuum was important for getting things done and winning the hearts and minds of others. Hence, she not only admitted her mistakes but shifted her own lead-ership style to one that was more collaborative and inclu-sive, which in many ways helped her to be a good senator and reinforces her platform today as secretary of state. Yet Hillary didn't dwell on her mistakes. That is the key to being resilient, as resilient people don't stay in the valley and keep reinforcing what they did wrong. Rather, they are transparent; they let people know what they learned and how they will turn the weakness into an opportunity and do better the next time around, and then they move on.

By doing this, you are less vulnerable in difficult situations or with people who challenge what you are doing. It also helps you to regulate your emotions when you find something that you don't like about yourself. It's this self-acceptance that helps you to eliminate distractions and self-doubt when you need to be resilient and self-sustaining as a leader.

To help you do this, spend time with people who know, believe, and trust you for who you are. Develop a small cadre of people who can be your sounding board in terms of how to leverage your strengths and mitigate your weaknesses in challenging situations. They can also help you to refine your boundaries—how far you can go before you are in conflict with your authentic self.

Remember that being authentic and acting in ways that are true to yourself as a leader can drive out fear because you are acting consistently based on your values and your strong beliefs. This will give you an amazing sense of freedom and resilience to tackle even the most difficult situations.

⸸ SECRET 2: WALK THE TALK ⸸

There is no question that Hillary has transformed herself as a leader over the years. Her work and her marriage often took her away from familiar ground and forced her to adapt and adopt. Yet with all these changes in her life, she has maintained her authenticity by staying on course with her true values and core beliefs, including her dedication to specific causes that she has supported since her early days at Wellesley: health care, women's rights, and child care. This may well be what led her to choose a life of public service. Reggie Van Lee, senior executive of health services at Booz Allen Hamilton, has had the opportunity to work with Hillary on various policy issues over the years. He shared with me that one of the biggest factors in Hillary's authenticity is her ability to hold on to her convictions in spite of challenges. He has witnessed her doing this both on a daily basis and throughout her career. One example he cited was health care. After putting her heart and soul into the health-care issue as first lady and being unsuccessful, she still worked vigorously on health-care reform nearly a decade later as a senator. I think this exemplifies how you show your authenticity by staying the course and continuing to "walk the talk" over time. While it's easy for you as a leader to become distracted from the things you believe in and care about, it's important that you maintain your focus and continue to act in accordance with them.

Take the time to ask yourself:

- What are my intrinsic motivations—those internal drivers that have been consistent throughout my life?
- Why are these most important to me?
- How have my actions over the past six months been aligned with or supported them?
- Have I done anything in the past six months that would cause others to think that I have abandoned something that I told them was important or critical for success?

Being authentic by following your core values and principles and by acknowledging your internal drivers can be difficult when you are pressured to think or act in a way that is in conflict with what you believe and feel. This can make you feel isolated and alone, so surround yourself with people who know your intentions and believe in you as a leader.

Finally, leading while being consistent with who you are often calls for speaking the truth. In politics or business today, we sometimes feel pressured to say things in order to please others or to look good in front of our colleagues. Authentic leaders are different. They consistently speak the truth. They would never betray themselves by using words that are not aligned with their values and actions. This does not give anyone a license to say things that are hurtful to people. Speaking the truth is simply about being clear, being honest, and being authentic.

⊹ SECRET 3: EXPRESS YOUR TRUE SELF ⊹

I can't say that Hillary's true self, particularly her emotional side, showed up in the earlier days of her career; however, from the 1960s through the early 1990s, women often had to adopt the more decisive, directive, and confrontational style known as a male style of leadership if they were to be taken seriously. Perhaps that explains why Hillary was known for her hard veneer, strong will, calculated action, and great perseverance rather than for her warm personality.

One of the most public expressions of Hillary's true self was when she spoke at a campaign rally in New Hampshire in 2008. While she was answering questions from the audience, she had a personal moment where she shed a few tears—to everyone's surprise. No one, with the exception of Hillary's close friends and family, had really seen Hillary's deeper sense of emotions and expressions from the heart come out. What the general population saw was her standing behind a podium speaking to larger crowds, or under the lights on TV and being drilled by the media. This expression of her true self is partially being driven, strong-willed, and focused on what she is working toward, but she is also someone who has a human side, which is expressed by her heartfelt emotions and her capacity to be vulnerable with others. This other expression of Hillary enabled her to truly connect with the audience, which was made up primarily of women.

Whether this emotional moment was due to extreme fatigue from the grueling campaign schedule, as some have suggested, or whether Hillary simply revealed her heartfelt feelings about her commitment to making this country a better place, this personal reaction created a new perception of her among women throughout the country. Suddenly, they saw that inside this tough-as-nails political candidate was a real person with the same vulnerabilities that they had. Soon after this happened, the polls indicated that Hillary had gained a majority of the women's vote, primarily because women could now identify with her more than they could with the other candidates.

When Hillary started to be more expressive, she realized that people liked that part of her. She began to talk more publicly about her personal side, which included everything from her family upbringing and her motherly instincts to many other personal experiences and lessons learned that were pivotal in shaping the person she is today.

She also began to show another side of herself, which was the fun, humorous, and personal woman that she is at the core. One example that illustrated this was when she was a guest on the *Late Show with David Letterman*. While she was a little nervous, knowing that talk-show guests can sometimes get skewered, she hoped that it would be fun and that she could let her true self come out. Her comeback to David Letterman made the audience roar with laughter, and Hillary said in her own words that she actually had a good time. That one TV talk show created a surprising shift in how many people viewed her, which was as more of the human and fun-loving person that she is.

While you and I may not want to shed tears in public, being able to connect with others by sharing our authentic thoughts and feelings, as well as our personal stories, improves and deepens our relationships, enabling us to gain the respect and trust of others. The key is knowing that there is a time and place to be expressive, and then giving yourself permission to share a piece of who you are by reflecting your heartfelt feelings about a situation or about yourself.

When I coach leaders on ways to engage with their employees, particularly during hard or challenging times, I always recommend that they first relay their own personal sadness, vulnerabilities, and fears. Once people know this part of who you are and your own feelings, they are more willing and able to connect with you, see you as a real person, and end up having a greater level of respect and support for you. This also builds a level of trust and a common bond that can go a long way. It creates a level of transparency that people appreciate and can connect with. In summary, you need to balance your intellect and logic with emotion. It's all about letting people know that you are confident enough to share your true self with them. That's life, that's being human, and that's being authentic.

⊹ SECRET 4: CREATE YOUR ⊹ PERSONAL BRAND

A direct correlation to your authentic self is your personal brand. Companies spend millions of dollars branding themselves because their brand—and people's perception of that brand—is their livelihood. They build their brand, nurture it, protect it, and defend it. And when necessary, the company will *rebrand* itself to respond to challenging times by changing established perceptions in order to be more successful.

In the same way, our personal livelihoods depend on our brand as a leader. The perception that our colleagues, bosses, and customers have of us plays a large role in the opportunities and promotions that come our way. If, at this stage of your career, you've got the brand you want, congratulations! But if you haven't got it just right, you need to rebrand yourself. Rebranding yourself can be challenging, since long-held beliefs about you can be difficult to change; but with some hard work, you can shake things up, change those unwanted perceptions, and create a new personal brand that will help you reach your goals.

When coaching both men and women business leaders about branding themselves, I encourage them to begin by identifying their core strengths. These strengths, when demonstrated consistently, can coalesce into a personal brand. In particular, look for those strengths that are unique to you—that help you to stand out in a crowd. I refer to these as your signature strengths; they are most likely to be things that you truly love doing, do exceptionally well, and probably do intuitively by now—all leading up to your authentic self.

When you know your signature strengths and lead with them, your brand will follow. You will be in control of what others think and say about you. Here are a few questions to consider when defining your authenticity through your personal leadership brand:

1. What are the four or five things that you want people to say about you when they are describing you as a leader? What exactly do you want them to mention or describe about you?
2. What specific opportunities do you have at work to create those particular impressions? Where do you "show up" as your leadership brand?
3. How much time and attention are you giving to the planning and preparation required to create these perceptions of you? Are you truly being intentional?
4. Are you consistently creating those impressions in meetings? With your colleagues? During presentations? In your e-mails?

5. Whom do you want to be associated with in your organization? Although discussing this is often controversial, your brand as a leader is also formed by whom you know and how "connected" other people think you are.

Finally it's important not to operate in a vacuum. You need to get feedback on the perception that people have of you now and what you have done to create those impressions in order to determine what you will need to do to change them. Seek out people you trust to coach you through this process. Invite people to watch you in action to see how you are projecting the qualities you want to be known for. What do you say? How do you carry yourself? What is the tone you use? When are you "being" your desired brand as a leader, and why and how are you showing up that way? With this information, you will be equipped to create a powerful brand for yourself.

⊹ SECRET 5: TELL YOUR OWN STORY ⊹

The word *authentic* is similar to the word *author*, which means that you are the author of your own story. We all have a book we can write, as we all have unique experiences, events, and even failures that have shaped who we are today. Leaders who acknowledge and appreciate their personal story have a natural sense of pride and self-acceptance. They are able to relate who they are today to specific experiences and influences in their lives. They can tell stories about both their opportunities and their challenges, their failures and their successes, and their moments of great joy along with their periods of great disappointment or sorrow. They recognize the specific people whom they admired and who greatly influenced them, and those who changed their thoughts and opinions about the things in life that are most important to them. They can laugh at themselves as they look back on their incorrect assumptions or valiant efforts that went awry. They can empathize with others who are suffering as they look back to their own periods of pain or loss. And they realize that without their story, no matter what it was, they wouldn't be the leaders they are today.

But just as important, they are not afraid to share their story with others. And as I listen to many of the stories told by business leaders, I am reminded that authentic leaders tell their story more in terms of what they have learned, cared about, or stood for than in terms of the positions they have held or the awards they have won. They use their story to show that they understand or to make a point rather than just to talk about themselves. They use it to connect with others and to invite others into their lives. Some stories are funny; some are sad. Some are long, and some are short. All of your stories are part of your authenticity, and each one differentiates you from everyone else.

When I speak on resilience and the importance of authenticity for leaders today, I often ask the audience what their story would be if they met someone going up in the elevator and had only three minutes with that person. Besides having your life story, it is also important to have the "sound-byte" version. This short and targeted version should help people gain a better sense of what's important to you, what you stand for, and what differentiates you from others.

In *Living History,* Hillary shares her story up front, which illustrates who she is today. She leads with,

> I was raised to love my God and my country, to help others, to protect and defend the democratic ideals that have inspired and guided free people for more than a hundred years. These ideals were nurtured in me as far back as I can remember. My childhood in the 1950s and the politics of the 1960s awakened my sense of obligation to my country and my commitment to service. My involvement on the ground floor of two presidential campaigns and my duties as First Lady took me to see every state in our union and to seventy-eight nations. In each place, I met someone or saw something that caused me to open my mind and my heart and deepen my understanding of the universal concerns that most humanity shares.

Every person has a story. It's a matter of taking the time to connect the dots between your past and your future to determine the essence of your life story, which will serve as a powerful vehicle for letting others know your passions, strengths, and values that enable you to lead with authenticity.

Like Hillary, we all have and continue to experience a journey of our lives that continues to affect who we are and what we stand for. The stories of great leaders focus less on their job title, whom they know, and their extrinsic rewards and more on what got them to where they are. It's more why they are doing what they are based on their past experiences that helps to create a context for their role as a leader and as an authentic human being. For Hillary, it was her rich experiences, her challenging times, and the extraordinary stretches she made on her own that created and shaped who she is and what she does today. For Hillary, it's not the job title or the monetary rewards that makes her unique and powerful but her overriding desire and passion to serve her country and to be a voice and vehicle for positive change, whether for families, education, or health care or as a catalyst for improving cooperation, relationships, and partnerships around the world.

Here are some steps to help you begin to define your story:

1. From early childhood on, what were the significant events, experiences, successes, failures, and people that had an impact on your life?

2. Which of these helped to shape your values? What were your top five values?
3. What were key events or turning points that helped you to develop your current vision and goals?
4. When your top five values were in conflict during your life, what did you do to get back on track?
5. Based on your life's journey, what are the goals and priorities that you are working on now?

In conclusion, I want you to know that your story continues in the hearts and minds of others when you leave. Authentic leaders leave a legacy. Success is wonderful, but significance is even better. You were made to contribute and to leave a mark on the people around you. When you fail to live from the frame of reference that your story gives you, you betray yourself. Authentic leaders are constantly telling their stories and building their legacies by adding deep value to the lives of others and leaving the world a better place in the process.

Consider the questions in this chapter to be an initial baseline for gauging your authenticity. There may be some areas that you feel good about and other areas that you would like to focus on now. Here are the five secrets again.

SECRETS FOR AUTHENTICITY

Secret 1: Accept who you are as a leader.

Secret 2: Walk the talk.

Secret 3: Express your true self.

Secret 4: Create your personal brand.

Secret 5: Tell your own story.

CHAPTER 5

IN TRANSITION— GAME CHANGER

Embracing Change

I'm sure you've heard this before, but I think it's worth saying again, "The one thing that is constant in life is change." And if you are a business leader today, you might be living this statement on a daily basis. Think of all the things we are "redoing" in organizations now, such as restructuring, resizing, reengineering, and retooling. Real leadership is not about leading in a "business as usual" environment but rather about leading during times that are tough and ambiguous—during times of change, like those that we are experiencing now.

While change has actually become a way of life in business over the past decade, it still seems to present us with difficult challenges. In fact, did you know that change remains the number one derailer of business executives? According to a study conducted by the Center for Creative Leadership (CCL), the primary reason that senior leaders fail is that they are "unable to deal effectively with change or adapt during a period of transition." That's the bad news. The good news is that this same study identified resiliency as being a key factor in a leader's ability to succeed during times of great change. So, what I want to focus on in this chapter is how you can embrace change as another opportunity to demonstrate your value as a resilient leader.

One of the keys to doing this is recognizing that in order to successfully lead others through change, you must first be able to embrace change in your own life. What Hillary once said about our nation is also true about each of us: "The challenges of change are always hard. It is important that we begin to unpack those challenges . . . and realize that we each have a role that requires us to change and become more responsible for shaping our own future."

A common pitfall for business leaders is not embracing personal change but rather continuing to rely on old behaviors and skills, even when they are no longer working. I remember coaching an executive who was struggling to succeed during a significant organizational restructuring effort. The company was trying to break down the existing "silos" and shift to a matrix structure to create a cross-collaborative work environment. This executive was very traditional, somewhat autocratic, and not a particularly good team player. When we first started working together, he described his day as "constantly walking into walls." Nothing seemed to make sense to him anymore. And yet, he continued to do what he had always done, expecting to get different results. Fortunately, with a little coaching, he was able to step back, access situations from another perspective, and make different choices. This took some work since he had to reevaluate his own assumptions, behaviors, and leadership style and determine which of these were causing him to hit the wall again and again. This greater awareness of himself helped him to make some important shifts. He first renewed his own vision for change for himself and for the organization and then began to adapt his style and communication methods, resulting in his becoming much more effective for implementing the "right" change in the organization.

But this wasn't easy for him. And it didn't happen overnight. The same is true of leading any significant change effort within your organization. It takes determination, focus, and hard work to make change happen. In the New Hampshire presidential debates, Hillary stated, "Making change is not about what you believe. It's not about a speech you make. It's about working hard." She then said, "What we need is someone who can deliver change. There are 7,000 kids in New Hampshire who have insurance because I helped to create the Children's Health Insurance Program. There's 2,700 National Guard and Reserve members who have access to health care because . . . I pushed legislation through . . . over the threat of a veto by President Bush." She was successful because she was persistent, and she worked hard to overcome the obstacles to change. Most change efforts that fail don't do so because people don't know what to change or don't have the right solution. They fail because people underestimate the amount of effort it takes to implement and sustain the change.

The following secrets focus on how to both personally embrace and professionally deliver change.

SECRET 1: RECOGNIZE THE HUMAN FACTOR IN CHANGE

As human beings, we all get into a pattern in terms of how we think, what we assume, and how we behave that can potentially limit our ability to see the need for change. Add to that the fact that change can be disorienting, uncomfortable, and even scary, and the result is a natural resistance to change. The best way to counter this negative reaction is to understand the normal phases that people go through when they are faced with change that affects them personally.

Think of a time when you experienced significant change, whether it was in your personal life or at work. Most likely, even if you were excited about the possibility of what was ahead, you went through a process of feeling awkward, scared, and maybe even sad, but you eventually felt less stressed and happier when you got closer to the "new" normal. When my company consults with organizations that are going through major change efforts, we map out the change itself and link it to the different phases that individuals will go through. This is a science that is tied directly to human behavior. If you understand these phases, you will have greater success in coping with and making the transition through each of the phases of the transformation process.

William Bridges, an organizational change expert, has identified three phases that people go through when they are dealing with a transition from an old way to a new way of doing things. These are *Endings*, *Exploration*, and *New Beginnings*.

During the Endings phase, people feel and must deal with their sense of personal loss. They often experience some level of anger, withdrawal, sadness, and frustration as well as resistance. They may be more focused on the past than on the future. There are some who will eventually tap into their resilience and begin to see the benefits of the change; however, this is usually an internal conversation rather than a time when someone takes action.

Before Hillary could run for the U.S. Senate seat, she had to experience an ending, which was the conclusion of her role as first lady. This was a reflective time for Hillary, as she shared in her book *Living History*. She wrote that being in the White House for eight years tested her faith, her political beliefs, and her marriage. She also acknowledged that while she and Bill had made their fair share of mistakes, she felt better because she knew that America was a stronger, better, and more just nation as a result of their efforts. We all deal with endings in different ways, but for Hillary, this was a time for her to reflect on both the negative and the positive aspects of her experience and to review what she had gained in terms of additional knowledge and wisdom. Then she gave herself permission to bring what she had learned from those experiences into her next role—whatever that would be. What a wonderful way to move through the Endings phase!

Exploration is the second phase of transition, and it typically introduces an entirely different set of issues for people. Once people have gotten many of their "me issues" resolved, the next set of issues tends to center on "who am I now?" People who are in Exploration are more concerned about the present, and their energy is invested in evaluating their options and searching for solutions.

When Hillary left the White House as first lady and began her senatorial campaign, she spent months learning how to become relevant to the people of New York State and how to differentiate herself from her opponent. This campaign role was something that she had never personally done before, and, as all people do while moving through the Exploration stage, she began to discover her new skill sets in mastering the intricacies of local politics and the dramatic differences between the personalities, cultures, and economies of upstate New York and the New York City suburbs. She referred to this phase as a "nonstop crash course" in New York and all its issues. She said in her own words, "I was discovering my capacities and limits for life as a political candidate. And I was finally moving beyond my role as a surrogate campaigner and allowing myself to operate on my own." Even though it was a steep learning curve for Hillary, by staying the course, she provided us with a great example of what happens when you identify your options during a major change and begin to make new choices for yourself. This is when you can begin to carve out a role for yourself as a change agent. You can look to see what needs to happen and determine how you might lead those particular efforts.

In the final stage of change, called New Beginnings, people begin to have the energy and attention to look outside themselves and begin to focus on others.

During an organizational change, they begin to notice that regular routines are being reestablished, that people have started figuring out how to get work done under the new conditions, and that social networks that make people feel more stable and connected are being reestablished. They begin to see how they can help others who are in a similar situation and how they can contribute to their success. Hillary's resilience, hard work, and commitment to moving through this significant change in her life successfully enabled her to get to this stage fairly quickly. You can do the same thing by taking a visible role as a change agent.

✠ SECRET 2: NEVER RESIST A ✠ GOOD CHANGE—GET AHEAD OF IT

It's normal to initially be wary of any major change, but now that you understand the human factor of change, you can take steps to move through the natural resistance phase as quickly as possible. Then, your opportunity to add value as a resilient leader depends on your ability to get ahead of the change.

Remember that being a resilient leader encompasses being adaptable and flexible. It assumes that you are comfortable with change and are open to things like a reorganization or a new way of doing things. It assumes that you want to learn about the changing conditions and be proactive in your response to them. But you can't do any of this if you are resisting the change.

If you are experiencing change and can feel yourself resisting it, ask yourself these questions:

- Am I reluctant to support the change effort?
- Is my resistance more than just an initial reaction to it?

- Do I feel that I will be losing something?
- Am I afraid that I will be giving up something that I am "famous for"?
- Am I being inflexible in terms of adapting to a new situation?
- Am I avoiding having to learn new ways of doing something?
- Am I afraid of failing as a result of this change?
- Are others coming to me to complain about the change?
- Am I hesitant to ask management about the change?
- Do I feel as if I have to wait to be asked to help with the change rather than taking the initiative myself?

If you answered yes to any of these questions, I encourage you to think twice about the way you are viewing the change and your role in the change process. In most cases, your assumptions and beliefs have probably been hardwired in your head and might need to be reexamined. Remember that not dealing with the core of your resistance could limit your chance to become the change agent that you are capable of being.

I remember that when I was a young kid, my brother and I would go sailing every weekend at our lake house in Indiana. What sailing taught me is that you can't wait to respond to the change in the wind; you have to anticipate it and make adjustments before you hit the changing conditions. In sailboat races, this meant looking at the boats ahead of us and determining where they were getting the optimum sail based on the path of the wind or how their sails were flapping in the wind. Then, the key was using that insight to adjust our course successfully. To me, this is a great metaphor for embracing change.

You need to be looking for signs that change is coming and then adapt your attitude and actions so that you are part of it rather than just feeling the effects of it. Show your interest by asking questions, then demonstrate your leadership by volunteering to do something that will move the change effort forward.

✠ SECRET 3: FOCUS ON WHAT YOU ✠ CAN CONTROL AND BE REALISTIC IN YOUR EXPECTATIONS

During a transition, we often feel that the things that we *can't* control are expanding and those that we *can* control are shrinking. As a result, we feel like victims, and we begin to blame others or make excuses for ourselves. Even if our perception is not accurate—and often it isn't—when we feel like victims, our energy is focused on what we might lose, and we feel threatened. To counter this negative reaction to change, it helps to focus on those things that we can control. By doing this, we are better able to use our time productively and to stay positive about future possibilities. In fact, sometimes when we "let go" and give up some of our control, new opportunities open up for us. In many cases, we are able to expand our knowledge in other areas, learn new ways of doing things, and possibly even get clearer about what is really important to us at the end of the day.

The best way to get to the root of this perception problem is to take a realistic look at what you actually have to simply accept as a result of the change or transition, and what you still control or can influence.

Here are some questions to help you do this.

- What are the things that I can't control about this change? Who is making these decisions? Why might they be doing what they are doing? How might I benefit from this change?
- If I lose control of these things, what's the worst that can happen?
- What are some things that I can control? How can I influence these aspects of the change?
- What can I do immediately to take advantage of the situation?
- Who can help me to figure things out and put together a plan of action that moves me in a positive direction?

When you begin to explore new possibilities and/or set new goals, it is important that you set expectations that are realistic and attainable so that the effort won't seem so overwhelming and you can see progress in the form of incremental steps. It is important for you to have some "short-term wins," whether you are dealing with a personal or an organizational change.

And, you should anticipate a few bumps along the way. It's normal to have some breakdowns in communication and some misunderstandings despite our best efforts to avoid them, and it's very common to have to make some midcourse corrections, no matter how good a plan you have, because circumstances change as you begin to better understand the particular situation. We may not be able to anticipate all of the problems ahead, but if we are realistic in our expectations, we can begin to anticipate some issues and map out, in general terms, how we will deal with them.

⊹ SECRET 4: CREATE AND SHARE ⊹ YOUR VISION FOR THE FUTURE

A vision, simply stated, is a picture painted in words that describes the desired result of the change effort. It helps people to see how the change will lead to a "better" tomorrow. You use a vision to gain the support of others and engage them in the change process.

Creating a clear, concise, consistent, and compelling vision for a change initiative is easier for some people than for others. I don't think anyone can dispute that Hillary has created a clear vision for U.S. foreign policy in her role as secretary of state. As it was reported in the *Washington Post* on August 3, 2009, she is leaving behind the old foreign relations doctrines and labels. She explained her vision by saying, "We envision getting not just a new group of states around a table, but also building networks, coalitions and partnerships of states and nonstate actors to tackle specific problems." Her major theme for change will emphasize "partnerships," "engagement," and "common interests," which means that the United States will be encouraging emerging global powers to be full partners in tackling the global agenda. This is a vision that her predecessors did not have when their efforts centered around the world's superpowers. We can see the change in her perspective and, she hopes, can anticipate a more positive future as a result of it.

If you are going to be an agent of change, you too need to craft your vision and be able to describe it so that others can connect with it. For example, for an organizational change, it's important that in your vision, you state the new growth opportunities and the "better" future that will result from the change. It's also important that you share how the old way of doing things does not fit into the bigger picture or will not allow the organization to reach its goals.

A strong change leader is out there on the front lines, communicating the rationale for change and explaining what others can realistically expect, both short- and long-term. Along with emphasizing the benefits of the change, the leader also explains how it will affect individuals and teams, how long the process of change will take, and what he will be doing during each phase of the transition. By managing people's expectations, it allows people to take more responsibility for dealing with the cycles of change effectively.

It's important that you use every vehicle possible to communicate both the new vision and the supportive strategies, such as town halls, e-mail, podcasts, brown-bag lunches, and one-on-one conversations. The message needs to be the same each time you deliver it, and people need to hear it over and over again if they are to believe that the change is actually going to happen and that it will be sustained over time. It also helps to give lots of examples and tell personal stories, as people remember these better than they remember general statements. Such stories also ensure better understanding and greater interest, which is what you are trying to achieve. Be creative and be enthusiastic, but also be authentic. People need to trust you if they are going to trust in your vision.

⊹ SECRET 5: COMMUNICATE! ⊹ COMMUNICATE! COMMUNICATE!

Remember that I said that times of change can provide you with great opportunities to showcase your skills as a resilient leader? Well, one of the areas in which you can really differentiate yourself is in your communication. Here are two things that you can do to be recognized as a strong communicator.

The first is to have the ability to speak clearly and concisely about the change effort, and then link it to others in a way that engages them. I call this your "elevator speech." Imagine that you meet someone in your organization on the ground floor of the building, and you are going to take the elevator to the tenth floor together. (I believe that takes about 90 seconds in most buildings.) Suppose that person says, "What are you working on now?" You want to have a well-crafted response that you can customize on the spot for anyone that you happen to be talking to. Here is a three-part formula for an elevator speech. While you will need to adapt it to your particular change effort, it is important that you cover all three parts if you want others to see you as a change agent.

Here's what the project is about:

- Here's why it's important to do it:
- Here's what success will look like:
- Here's what we need from you:

Second, if you are leading a change effort, you need to have a communication plan. The purpose of the plan is to get the right *information* to the right *people* at the right *time* in the right *way* (mode).

It's important to determine both who *needs* to know something and who *wants* to be kept in the information loop. Other than the obvious exception for situations that involve confidentiality, it is good to determine who the key stakeholders are and plan how and when you will communicate with them. Key stakeholders are those people who will be directly or indirectly affected by the change and people who can affect the decisions that are going to be made about the change effort.

When determining your message, keep in mind what you are trying to achieve by your communication. Are you informing others so that something happens as a result of their gaining certain information? Are you trying to influence others to think or feel a certain way or to do something? Are you trying to reduce the uncertainty and ambiguity regarding the change? Are you trying to get out in front of the "gossip" to reduce the anxiety? Are you trying to promote the benefits of the change by reiterating your vision? If you know what you want to happen as a result of your communication, you are better prepared to craft your message.

When to communicate is a factor of what you are communicating. In general, I think it's best to communicate about change sooner rather than later. However, it's important that you have enough of the details so that people feel that the change is well thought out and that those responsible for making it happen know what they are doing. The exception is when you are informing people so that they can do something as a result of gaining specific information. In those situations, it is better to give them the specific information closer to when they actually have to apply it. And remember that communication needs to be ongoing. The way people hear it the first time will be different from the way they hear it the next time, as they gradually begin to realize how the change will affect them and their team or organization.

Finally, it's important to use multiple media to communicate and to engage in two-way communication throughout the change process. Hillary has become very adept at this. From her town hall meetings, to her televised debates and interviews, to her messages delivered on YouTube and her e-mails sent to supporters, she has leveraged every communication mode available to her.

In Hillary's foreign policy address, she reinforced the importance of making every effort to communicate with people from the bottom up. She said, "In every country I visit I look for opportunities to bolster civil society and engage with citizens, whether at a town hall in Baghdad, a first in that country, or appearing on local popular television shows that reach a wide and young audience, or meeting with democracy activists, war widows, or students." This is a minor change in our foreign policy, but she communicates it in order to reinforce the general change in her approach. You too need to use every mode available to reach and engage your key stakeholders.

Here is a quick self-check to see if you are open to change and if you are being an effective change agent in your role as a resilient leader.

⊹ HOW WILLING ARE YOU ⊹ TO EMBRACE CHANGE?

- Are you proactive in seeking out or anticipating change rather than waiting for change to happen and then responding to it?
- Are you flexible and adaptable, or are you more set in your ways and not comfortable adapting to changing conditions?
- When leading change, do you craft a vision that you communicate concisely and consistently in order to enroll others in the effort?
- When you lead others through a change effort, do you allow them to move naturally through the three different phases of change described in this chapter, or do you force them to move at a pace that you feel is expedient?
- When leading change, do you have a communication plan that focuses on the needs of stakeholders, in terms of what they both need and want to know?

SECRETS FOR EMBRACING CHANGE

Secret 1: Recognize the human factor in change.

Secret 2: Never resist a good change—get ahead of it.

Secret 3: Focus on what you can control and be realistic in your expectations.

Secret 4: Create and share your vision for the future.

Secret 5: Communicate! Communicate! Communicate!

CHAPTER 6

LISTENING
TOURS
Being Connected

S trategic networking is the best way to build relationships with others in order to improve the quality of your
work and get it done faster or to learn about job opportunities. Being connected takes this concept one step further
than just building a series of individual relationships, as
helpful as each of these relationships might be. *Being connected* means intentionally forming relationships with certain individuals or groups in order to create some kind of
positive action or an outcome that while it may benefit you,
will also benefit another person or even, in the best cases,
benefit the greater good. Although strategic networking is
a part of this, another important dimension of being con-

nected is building bridges by forming strategic alliances. I know this sounds complicated, but it really isn't, and it can actually be fun.

Let me give you an example. Several years ago, I met with a client who had the task of strengthening the pipeline of her organization's women leaders. The company was experiencing what it called "regrettable losses"—losing very talented women who went to work for another company in what appeared to be a lateral move. I convinced my client that people who feel personally connected to their colleagues are less likely to leave, unless another opportunity offers significantly more money or greater responsibility. As a result, our first step was to form a Women's Executive Committee, which represented all the different business units across the country, to discuss potential ways to address the key concerns and issues of the firm's current and future women leaders. We decided that the number one goal was to build a cross-supportive network for the women, where they could come together, get to know one another on a personal basis, share ideas, and even cross-mentor one another.

We started by hosting a single event where about 25 female leaders and executives were invited to a brown-bag lunch. The women sat around the table and shared who they were and what they did. Then they candidly discussed some of the unique opportunities and challenges that they faced on a daily basis. This exchange was powerful for many of the women in the room. In a very short amount of time, they were able to build common ground around some of the issues they faced and gain both important information and intriguing insights from one another. One important outcome of the session was that the women had the chance to listen and learn what their colleagues did, their key business objectives, and the challenges they faced. This dialogue enabled them to have a more cultivated perspective on the business and how they all connected with and supported one another. This is key, particularly for women, as I hear many times from senior executives that one obstacle for women in advancing their careers is their lack of being strategic. This is primarily due to their not getting out and learning about the larger context of the business because of their assumed need to "do the work," which limits their ability to tap into other views and perspectives across and outside the organization.

Over the course of the year, we leveraged the success of this event by conducting satellite forums, an annual one-day leadership conference, and a series of Webinars, newsletters, and informal mentoring opportunities for women across the organization. This single idea of creating a network for women within this company evolved into a very successful program for women in the company worldwide. Not only has it served as a tremendous catalyst for women to see the value of advocating and mentoring each other, but it has also helped to create a greater sense of community among women in the company, which has dramatically improved the retention rates of women in leadership positions and in the leadership pipeline. This is what I mean by the power of being connected. While each of these women benefited individually from this strategic alliance, the organization also reaped the reward.

Hillary is a master at building networks and alliances for the greater good. She began to expand her own circle of relationships many years ago. Dee Dee Myers, press secretary for the Clinton administration, shared with me that early in Hillary's career, her inner circle was much smaller and consisted mainly of very supportive friends and family members. But as first lady in Arkansas and then in the White House, Hillary learned that she needed a broader and more diverse network of people whom she could use as a sounding board on important issues and who could actively help her have greater influence by gaining support from people who might normally be considered part of the opposition. Relationships of this kind are critical for gaining access to information rather than waiting for it to come to you or for tapping into people who have a high degree of knowledge, credibility, and respect on a certain issue and who can give you the advice you need and help you move that issue along. Dee Dee said, "Now, because Hillary's friends and colleagues are six degrees of separation with so many other people in the world, she has successfully created an incredibly broad and diverse sphere of relationships all around her."

Her friend and colleague Kristin Mannion describes Hillary as "the best" at reaching out to people who are not in agreement with her and convincing them that achieving the larger goal is more important than being defeated by their minor differences. In *Living History*, Hillary said, "As Senator, I tried to bridge the partisan divide by bringing Republicans and Democrats together whenever I could on issues ranging from homeland security to education to defense. I've reached out to political opponents, including a few who led the charge for my husband's impeachment!" She learned how to reach "across the aisle" to find common ground in order to work together for the good of the country.

Creating networks and making connections is not always about reaching out to allies. It's often about getting out of your comfort zone and breaking down traditional barriers to find a common purpose and set of intentions that mobilize others to get the "right" thing done for the "right" reasons.

I believe that there are two key things that separate successful business leaders from those who fail:

- The mindset that they *cannot* do it all alone
- The ability to build networks and alliances that provide them with both invaluable guidance to overcome obstacles and the necessary support to achieve critical goals

In her address to the Asia Society in February of 2009, as secretary of state, Hillary used this concept of "connectedness" to describe a new era in U.S. diplomacy. She said, "Today it is tempting to focus our attention on the tensions and perils of our interdependence, but I prefer to view our connectedness as an opportunity for dynamic and productive partnerships that can address both the challenge and the promise of this new century." Isn't this also true for resilient business leaders? We are living in a world that is getting more complex every day, and leaders need creative ideas and integrated thinking to solve problems and take advantage of opportunities. As a result, business is increasingly getting done through networks, partnerships, and alliances made up of very diverse individuals.

Finally, I want to delve into the idea of being connected in order to help others. Reaching out and supporting others unconditionally is a critical component of expanding your network and building powerful alliances. While the law of reciprocity says that if you help someone else, that person will owe you a favor in return, I think that there is more to it than that. I call it "generosity of the heart." People feel that you are a special person when you support them for the sake of their success or the achievement of a worthwhile goal, and for no other reason. I heard this over and over again about Hillary as I interviewed her friends and colleagues for this book. Kristin Mannion shared this with me:

Hillary does "reach out," but she also invites and seeks out people to exchange ideas and add value to whatever topic is under discussion. She is motivated intellectually to learn what she doesn't know, but should know, to better understand the issues at hand, and to try to get it right. She is not a person to make snap decisions, or believe that she is the only one with the right answer—she strives to capture facts, data, and perspectives to add to her own to arrive at solutions that have a better chance of succeeding at improving whatever situation she is addressing. Also, the board we *both* served on was called the Child Care Action Campaign, and it was in the 1980s. She was First Lady of Arkansas at the time, and I was working on Wall Street. I was serving as a committee chair and had to call upon her to help with a project. What I truly appreciated was her immediate responsiveness coupled with her honesty about what she could and could not do. She never overpromised, and she always came through with whatever she committed to do. It was truly productive to have a clear idea of what to count on, and then to know that none of the things that she had committed to would fall through the cracks. This helped all of us do the work that was necessary. She was always a direct, honest contributor to the thought process and to the tactical execution of a strategy or initiative. She stayed focused on what her best contribution was and always saw it through. She didn't do it for *me*, she did it for the *cause* that she believed in—I barely knew her then.

Kristin then expressed to me, "My heart was encouraged by her honesty and her keen sense of commitment to her offered help. And, of course, to the warmth and humor that she always brought along with her intellect and commitment. I was indeed lucky, later in life, to have reason to spend time with her, and to learn more from her as the years passed."

This story from Kristin was just one example of many that illustrated Hillary's openness and her intention to be of value to others. Of course, Hillary developed a host of new relationships as a result, but, best of all, she encouraged Kristin's heart in an effort that made a difference to others, and, in the process, she created a lasting impression. That's what I mean by being connected in order to help others.

So, now let's get to the secrets for building your connectedness. In order to build partnerships and alliances, you have to begin by expanding your network.

⌖ SECRET 1: DON'T BE AFRAID ⌖ TO ASK FOR HELP

When I interviewed dozens of business executives for my previous book, I learned that one of the things they had in common was the belief that they needed a strong network for advice and support. For example, when Anne Mulcahy was asked to move into the CEO role at Xerox, she was inheriting an organization that had lost market share and whose sales were at a dangerously low point. One of the first things she did was to meet with her top 100 managers to gain their insights, and then she picked up the phone and called Warren Buffett, whom she didn't know personally, and asked for his advice as well. Based on their collective input, she put together a business development strategy that she was confident would be successful, and it was.

The lesson here is that you can't figure it all out and do it all by yourself. You need to have contacts to call upon, both inside and outside your organization. And then you need to have the courage to ask for their help. Now, I realize that this is easy for some of us to do, but, believe me, it's not so easy for everyone. I know of many leaders who want to seek advice or ask for support, but just can't make themselves pick up the phone and make that call. They fear that the other person is too busy, or that the person will say yes to be polite, but then won't follow through, or—even worse—they are afraid that the other person will think that they are less confident or competent because they asked for help. But, does this really happen? Think of a time when someone asked you for help. How did you feel, and how did you respond? Most people feel flattered and will help as much as they can.

And getting a positive response is not just about the other person. Sometimes the result of the request lies in the *asking*. You should know exactly what you want the other person to do for you. Often, after I've been on a panel at a conference, I invite attendees to visit my Web site and send me a question, which I am always glad to answer, either personally or in my next blog. You wouldn't believe how difficult it sometimes is for me to figure out exactly what the person sending me the question really wants to know. And the same thing happens when someone comes up to me after I've given a presentation. Many times people think that I can help them, but they are not clear about what they want from me, and in those situations I usually don't have time to try to help them figure it out. The same thing happens when you ask someone in your network for help. You need to make it easy for that person to say yes by being clear about what you want or are asking her to do for you.

It's also important to consider the best way to make your request. Here's the rule that I have found to be most reliable: ask in a way that will play to the other person's style. If the other person is an introvert and likes to think about things before he responds, send him an e-mail and ask for a time when you can discuss it with him. If the person is an extrovert, you might want to just pick up the phone or walk into her office and discuss it with her informally.

Here are a few questions that will help you to clarify your request:

- What is the situation, and why is it important?
- What exactly do you want this person to do for you?
- Why are you asking this person for this help rather than someone else?
- What is the benefit to you, this person, and the greater good?

⊹ SECRET 2: BUILD A BROAD ⊹ AND DIVERSE NETWORK

Each of us has a network. These are the folks we go to for advice and support. The first thing I want you to do is identify the people in your current network. If you have never done this before, start by identifying groups of people. For example, common groups usually include family, friends, work colleagues, customers or clients, clubs or associations, church, volunteer organizations, and so on. List every person that you know in a particular group, and then put a check mark beside each person that you feel you could call to ask for help. These are considered to be in your *active* network. The people without check marks are your *potential* network. These are people that you are connected to indirectly, and they are often the easiest people to reach out to in the future to bring them into your active network.

Here are a few questions to help you analyze your network:

- Are most of the people in your network people whom you've known for a long time or whom you work with on a daily basis, or are they a combination of people inside and outside your organization who come from different walks of life, with different experiences, perspectives, and professions?
- Does your network include people at a more senior level as well as peers and direct reports?
- Is it diversified by age, gender, nationality, race, industry, geography, and other such factors?
- Does it include both long-term and short-term relationships?
- How many folks did you reach out to in order to originally build the relationship, and how many reached out to you?
- What are you doing to maintain these relationships? Do you make a conscious effort to stay in touch with people, or is it "out of sight, out of mind" for you?
- What would you like to do to reconnect with some of these folks?

Now, I want you to think outside the box and consider people who are not currently in your network. Think beyond the group of people who are already committed to you and have been there for you in the past, and think beyond your potential network to identify people who can do one of two specific things for you: they can show you a very different perspective, or they can connect you with people whom you would not ordinarily meet within your current network.

I've already discussed the advantage of having different perspectives in order to find the most effective way to address today's business challenges, but let me explain why you might want to establish a relationship with someone who operates in very different circles from those in which you operate. One relationship in a new "community" can expand your network dramatically because that one person can connect you to anyone else in her network. I've mentioned attending several functions in Washington, D.C., that were hosted by Hillary. I attended because she has always fascinated me and I knew that there would be interesting people there and that the conversations would be memorable, but I also knew that I'd meet a broad spectrum of professionals with very different backgrounds and life experiences from those of the people that I ordinarily meet. In one room, I'd often find lawyers, doctors, politicians, teachers, scientists, and even philanthropists. I always tried to remember whom I met, and sometimes I even collected business cards. Then I'd go home and jot down when and where I met each person and what was memorable about him. I can't tell you how often, when someone asked me for help or when I needed to build a broad base of support for a business venture or for a cause I was supporting, I'd tap into those folks. When I called, I mentioned where and when we had met and what I remembered about that person, and then I explained why I was calling. That's called broadening your network.

Once you've expanded your strategic network—those relationships that you develop with intention—you can begin to think about building partnerships and alliances. Betsy Griffith, a close friend and classmate of Hillary's at Wellesley, said, "Hillary listens to a new or powerful idea, and then she takes that idea and networks it with other communities in order to improve upon it and to gain a broad base of support for it." Hillary calls this "smart power." In her address to the Council on Foreign Relations in July of 2009, she said, "Building the architecture of global cooperation requires us to devise the right policies and use the right tools. I speak often of smart power because it is so central to our thinking and our decision-making. It means the intelligent use of all means at our disposal, including our ability to convene and connect."

I believe that this approach reflects how leadership is evolving today, from a hierarchical approach with a single leader to a more inclusive approach with collaborative leadership.

⊹ SECRET 3: HAVE A PLAN ⊹

When you're building your network, it's important that you think strategically and be intentional about the relationships you will establish and the commitments you will make together. Remember to stretch your thinking and consider people both inside and outside of your specific organization. Be creative when you are thinking about ways to cultivate these relationships, and consider who else might be able to help you make the initial connection. Here is a simple framework for developing an action plan.

- What is your goal? What do you want to achieve? What will success look like?
- What do you need help doing?
- Who can best help you? (Consider several people.)
- Do you need to form a new relationship with each of these people or just reconnect with each so as to deepen or broaden your current relationship?
- What is the value in cultivating and sustaining these relationships? (Consider both the short term and the long term.)
- What specifically do you want each person to agree to do? (This can be as simple as getting to know each other or as complex as writing a recommendation for you!)
- What do you commit to do to engage each person? What are the specific actions that you will take, and by when?

When you are developing your action plan, think realistically about when you will be able to make time to focus on each individual. Also, try to put one person on the list who will be a "stretch" for you—someone who is a little out of your comfort zone. And, try to put another person on the list who can give you a totally different perspective. Finally, be sure to be clear about whether you are asking for help or making a suggestion for how the two of you can engage with each other. Do your homework and be prepared.

Once you are comfortable with this approach to building your network, I suggest that you begin to reach out to people just because you think they are interesting and you want to get to know them better. You can actually build these new relationships proactively and unconditionally. Get involved in outside activities, go to networking events, attend conferences, and even consider serving on a committee for a cause that you care about. When you meet someone that you would like to get to know better, let her know what you do and be very open about the fact that you would like to better understand what she does so that the two of you might be able to support each other in the future. When you do this, you begin to develop a common rapport and level of trust with that person, so that when you do ask her for help, she will be more open to supporting you.

⚜ SECRET 4: CREATE YOUR OWN ⚜ BOARD OF DIRECTORS

When I speak on the topic of building strategic networks, I always ask people if they have their own personal board of directors, much the way executives have a their small network of people whom they can count on for personal advice and support. These people are less like the traditional corporate board members or formal advisors than like a small group of friends and colleagues who know you well and have your best interests at heart.

These people are invaluable when you are trying to tackle a complex issue or when you need advice because you have a difficult choice to make. They are the ones who can help you develop a broader vision of yourself, reenergize you to stay the course by renewing your sense of purpose and commitment, or encourage you to move in an entirely new direction.

I have always had a board for my company. These seven business leaders meet with me several times a year to review my strategic business plan and advise me on issues such as how to stay competitive in challenging times and how to continue to grow my business in new and emerging markets. They have very different educational and experiential backgrounds and have been very successful in a variety of industries, so they provide me and my executive team with perspectives that we would not ordinarily have available to us.

But I also have my own personal board of directors. Several years ago, a friend asked me to dinner and explained that she was looking to make a career change and wanted me to help her think through it. She had invited five other people to join us, and she had an agenda for us to work though after dinner. When we all arrived, she referred to us as her personal board of directors. We chatted during dinner and then listened while she explained her situation and what she considered to be her options. We all contributed our ideas and shared insights from our own experiences. By the end of the evening, she had achieved her goal of thinking outside the box and was able to see her choices in a new light. I thought this idea of having a personal board was terrific, and I immediately created one of my own.

Because several of the folks I chose to be on my personal board lived far away from me, I approached each one individually, and we did much of our initial work together via the phone. I still reach out to them whenever I need a sounding board or just need someone to talk straight with me about something. Over the years, I have helped hundreds of others to create their own personal boards, and the results have been incredible. You might want to consider doing this for yourself as you are getting connected in terms of your role as a resilient leader. These relationships can be formed for a number of reasons. You may want to benchmark an idea that you have had, look at ways to expand your own business perspective outside your organization, or be connected to someone whom you don't know or whom you would value to gain some feedback on your role and your impact as a leader.

There are three things that you want to demonstrate when you reach out to others, whether you want them to be on your board or to be in your network. Here they are:

- *Authenticity*. Be yourself, and don't have any hidden agendas.
- *Integrity*. Have a pure motive, and be transparent.
- *Intention*. Have a clear goal in mind that you feel you can achieve with the other person.

If you keep these things in mind, you will thrive with your newfound connectedness, and you will be amazed at how the time and energy you put into this effort will help you, your organization, and the greater good of the community.

SECRET 5: BE OPEN TO AND CURIOUS ABOUT EVERYONE YOU MEET

You just never know when you will run into someone who can help you or who can connect you with others who will broaden your network in a dramatically different way. Don't assume that you have nothing in common with the airline stewardess. Sometimes the best connections are also the least expected.

Let me explain how I met a woman who enlarged my network by 10,000 people. I had just returned from San Francisco on a red-eye, and I was back on a 7 a.m. flight to

Orlando the next morning. The flight was packed, and I was thrilled that the seat beside me was empty. I pulled out my headphones and looked forward to taking a well-needed rest when a woman sat down next to me and immediately asked if I was the *Sticky Floor* lady whose book she was currently reading. I had a choice between nodding my head and closing my eyes (which every cell in my body was encouraging me to do!) or taking off my headphones and answering her politely. Luckily for me, my midwestern manners had me do the latter, and we introduced ourselves. She was the president of one of the largest lobbying firms in Washington, D.C., and she immediately asked me to speak at the firm's annual conference. As we continued our discussion about the conference, she asked me if I had a blog (which I do) and if I'd be interested in posting each other's blogs on our individual Web sites so that we could both expand our communities. By connecting with just one person, I added 10,000 people to my network!

Now, you might not be quite so lucky, and you may not even want to build a network that is called a community, but who knows what a brief conversation with someone new will turn into? So, be open and friendly with everyone you meet. Be curious about who that person is and what he is doing in the world. Be receptive to potential synergies and new opportunities that you can create together to support common goals. And be sure to note the person's name, his contact information, when and where you met, and what was memorable about him, just as you do when you are expanding your business network.

I've heard that there are no coincidences in life. People come into and out of your life for a reason. There are lessons to be learned and messages to be heard from everyone you meet. Are you listening? Are you connecting?

⚜ HOW WELL ARE YOU BUILDING ⚜ AND LEVERAGING YOUR CONNECTIONS?

- Do you normally reach out and ask other people for advice and support, or do you try to tackle things on your own?
- Do you have a broad and diverse spectrum of relationships in your active network, or are most of your relationships the same friends and colleagues that you have relied upon for some time now?
- Do you take time to leverage your network by creating linkages from one community to another, building cooperative partnerships to achieve the greater goal?
- Do you take the time to connect with others? Do you express true interest in their well-being and their ideas? Do you actively listen and withhold any judgment, with the intention of learning and being able to support them or connect their idea to another network or person?

- Do you take time to support others around you, unconditionally?

SECRETS FOR BUILDING YOUR CONNECTEDNESS

Secret 1: Don't be afraid to ask for help.

Secret 2: Build a broad and diverse network.

Secret 3: Have a plan.

Secret 4: Create your own board of directors.

Secret 5: Be open to and curious about everyone you meet.

CHAPTER 7

MAKING YOUR WORDS COUNT
Awesome Communication

In order to inspire a more resilient workforce and achieve real results in this business climate, leaders need to be *awesome* communicators. In addition to applying the basics of being clear, concise, consistent, and compelling when transferring factual information, you need to be able to successfully deliver many other messages that are intended to affect specific situations and individuals. And we all know how difficult it is to just do the basics.

Studies show that we spend close to 80 percent of our time communicating each day, and more than 60 percent of that communication is confusing, misconstrued, or even incorrect. This not only causes a great deal of confusion and frustration but also results in a significant lack of productivity. So, be sure to get some reliable feedback on your effectiveness in the basics. Then begin to hone your communication skills and techniques in order to make your words count when you are delivering those other messages.

By now you've read about many of these important messages in previous chapters. We've covered the importance of being able to share a vision that resonates with others and being able to express your true self by being emotionally expressive. In this chapter, I'd like to drill down in both of these areas. Then I'll cover several other key aspects of awesome communication, including how to

- Adapt your style to your audience.
- Listen with intention.
- Have those difficult conversations that you've been putting off.

Why is it important that you be able to do these other things well? That's easy. Being a resilient leader means being able to move people and projects forward in spite of obstacles and challenges. And, more than anything else, these communication secrets are the tools and techniques that enable us to do that: *inspire action, speak from your heart, adapt your style, listen with intention,* and *don't avoid the hard conversations.*

Hillary has an impressive capacity for the kind of communication I'm talking about. Based on what she said and how she said it, 18 million people were convinced that she was capable of being the president of the United States, and thousands were inspired to work actively for her campaign. But I don't think it was what she said during the campaign as much as what she said when the campaign was over and she wanted to inspire others to action to support her former adversary that really defined her as an awesome communicator.

At the 2008 Democratic National Convention, Hillary had a matter of minutes in which to convince her supporters, and the rest of the country, that she genuinely supported Obama and that they should, too. It must not have been an easy task when she had put so much hard work and all of her heart into a race that had ended so closely. Yet Hillary flexed her resilient leadership and delivered a speech that was intended to win the hearts and minds of her audience. She said, "I want you to ask yourselves: Were you in this campaign just for me? Or were you in it for that young Marine and others like him? Were you in it for that mom struggling with cancer while raising her kids? Were you in it for that boy and his mom surviving on the minimum wage? Were you in it for all the people in this country who feel invisible?" Then she paused and continued:

We need leaders once again who can tap into that special blend of American confidence and optimism that has enabled generations before us to meet our toughest challenges. Leaders who can help us show ourselves and the world that with our ingenuity, creativity, and innovative spirit, there are no limits to what is possible in America.

This won't be easy. Progress never is. But it will be impossible if we don't fight to put a Democrat in the White House.

We need to elect Barack Obama.

By the time she finished, the crowd was on its feet cheering for her and for her message. She had made her words count in an extraordinary way, and you can learn to do the same.

Her approach to communication was effective, based on creating visual pictures that hooked into and touched people's hearts. Her words and her approach helped to remind people of the importance of achieving their mutual goals together and that she was behind the greater goal for all.

Here are five secrets for awesome communication.

⊹ SECRET 1: INSPIRE ACTION ⊹

Let me begin by explaining the importance of the word *inspire* when we are talking about resilient leadership. Many leaders, such as those in the military, are effective in certain situations by ordering people what to do and when to do it. Because of their positional power, they most often get compliance from those they are leading. A resilient leader is looking for more than compliance. Hillary's goal is commitment that encourages people to act. I call this *inspiring* action.

Have you ever noticed that great leaders communicate in a very positive way? Even their tone conveys a "can do" attitude. And they use this empowering optimism in two ways: they focus on the positive aspects of people and on hopes for the future. On September 11, Rudy Giuliani, mayor of New York City, was addressing a city in crisis when he responded to a reporter's question about New Yorkers and how they were dealing with the terrorist attacks. Giuliani said, "They are just the most wonderful people in the world. We have without any doubt the best police department, fire department, the best police officers, the best fire officers, the best emergency workers of any place in the whole world." He then shifted and made his communication focus on the future. He said, "The people in New York City will be whole again. We are going to come out of this emotionally stronger, politically stronger, much closer together as a city, and we're going to come out of this economically stronger, too."

Hillary used this same kind of empowering optimism in her commencement speech at New York University when she said, "As secretary of state, I am well aware of the challenges that we face. You, as new graduates, and your generation will be up against those challenges. . . . But I am absolutely convinced that you and we are up to the task. . . . Our challenges are ones that summon the best of us, and we will make the world better tomorrow than it is today."

Hillary has a theme in much of her communication, and that theme is "We can do this! We can make this better!" During hard times, this is what people want and need to hear. It's the optimism and positive communication that reengages people, gives them hope, and motivates them to take some kind of action, as opposed to being the victims of unfortunate circumstances.

Another way to inspire action is to use the power of language to create a shared vision of the future. For example, Martin Luther King Jr., used a number of visual images in his speeches, such as "the prodigious hilltops of New Hampshire," "the heightening Alleghenies of Pennsylvania," and "a beautiful symphony of brotherhood." These examples create a mental picture that a diverse audience can identify with. We can all enrich our language by using stories, metaphorical expressions, and figures of speech to actually create visual images. I was told once that if we can picture it, and if we can put ourselves in that picture, we can make it happen.

But I don't want you to think that only superstars can do this. I remember coaching a business leader whose company's stock price was tanking. Morale was low, people were stressed, and many feared that they would soon lose their jobs. This business leader wanted to create a sense of hope and encourage resilience and commitment throughout his organization, and he knew that the usual business presentation of facts and figures wouldn't do that. So, we put together another approach.

He scheduled a "town hall" meeting, and we created two PowerPoint slides for it. The first slide showed a stream of valleys that kept dipping lower over the course of the year. The second slide showed a beautiful picture of mountains, with each one getting taller, and on the highest peak there was a circle indicating where the company was—at the top! As he addressed his team at the meeting, he showed the slides and explained that over the next several months, there would be hard times, and that they would all have to work hard, but that he firmly believed that their common values and strong work ethic would prevail. He spoke confidently when he said that they had the power to move beyond the current situation and that they would, together, reach the mountain peak that represented their shared vision for the company. Then he explained his short-term plan in order to provide them with some immediate direction, and finally he told them about a series of meetings he was going to hold to get everyone's ideas on the best way to move forward in the longer term. People are still talking about that meeting. They call it the "peak" meeting, and I call it inspiring action.

Here are some things to remember when you want to inspire action:

- Find a common ground for people with diverse backgrounds and interests by identifying common values, goals, aspirations, and dreams.
- Focus on the future in terms of what can and will be accomplished.
- Let people know that you understand their fears and concerns, but convey *empowering optimism* to encourage thinking about the possibilities.
- Use a variety of modes of expression (metaphors, stories, pictures, and so on) to make your message come alive.
- Speak positively and with confidence about the power of people and mutual aspirations. For example, replace "we will try" with "we will" and "we are."

✢ SECRET 2: SPEAK FROM YOUR HEART ✢

When we looked at authenticity, I addressed the importance of being emotionally expressive and sharing your true self with others. There is also a time and place to speak from your heart when you are leading people through times of change or challenging situations and you want them to feel personally connected to you and to your message.

One way to do this is to acknowledge the current situation, citing specific examples that demonstrate that you have listened to the people you are communicating with, have heard both their words and their emotions, and truly understand what they are telling you and how they are feeling about it. Often this means that you are talking about things like hopes and dreams or fears and pain. This is called having *empathy*. It's a major component of emotional intelligence. It not only demonstrates that you "get it" but also shows that you care enough about the other person to make sure that you "get it right."

Then you need to be able to show that you genuinely care deeply about the issue and that you are committed to making a difference. Each conversation is very personal, and it is not unusual for some of us to become emotional as we engage with others at this level. If it is genuine, the emotion is spontaneous and can be very powerful. But it cannot be faked or manufactured in order to have a certain effect. People know the difference.

Finally, you need to be able to move from the emotion to the inspiration. You need to close with your vision in a way that gives the other person confidence and moves her forward.

Going back to my example of Hillary's speech at the 2008 Democratic National Convention, you'll see what I mean. After demonstrating that she had listened to people on the campaign trail by citing key themes that she had heard, she got personal and shared how specific individuals had "touched her heart" with their stories. She said:

You taught me so much, you made me laugh, and . . . you even made me cry. You allowed me to become part of your lives. And you became part of mine.

I will always remember the single mom who had adopted two kids with autism, didn't have health insurance and discovered she had cancer. But she greeted me with her bald head painted with my name on it and asked me to fight for health care.

I will always remember the young man in a Marine Corps T-shirt who waited months for medical care and said to me: "Take care of my buddies; a lot of them are still over there . . . and then will you please help take care of me?"

I will always remember the boy who told me his mom worked for the minimum wage and that her employer had cut her hours. He said he just didn't know what his family was going to do.

I will always be grateful to everyone from all fifty states, Puerto Rico, and the territories, who joined our campaign on behalf of all those people left out and left behind by the Bush Administration.

To my supporters, my champions—my sisterhood of the traveling pantsuits—from the bottom of my heart: Thank you.

And then she came back with a charge to the troops to get Barack Obama elected in order to address these challenges and have hope for the future. This is what I mean when I say to *speak from your heart*. Hillary expressed her personal feelings and was speaking from a human and emotional perspective rather than giving facts and speaking more rationally.

To summarize how to speak from the heart when you want to have others connect with your message, here are the three steps: (1) demonstrate that you understand what people are saying and how they are feeling, (2) show that you care and are committed to making a difference by sharing on a personal level, and then (3) move from emotion to inspiration. It might sound complicated at first, but once you begin to use this approach, it will become intuitive. And, your communication will be awesome.

⊹ SECRET 3: ADAPT YOUR STYLE ⊹

As we mature as leaders, we have a host of different experiences that eventually help us home in on certain leadership approaches that seem to naturally work best for us. We call these approaches a *preferred leadership style*. For some of us, it is being more directive in our management style. For others, it is being more collaborative, or more of a visionary, and so on. In Carl Bernstein's book *A Woman in Charge*, he describes Hillary's leadership style as one that creates a nurturing culture of collegiality and loyalty that is based on teamwork, a style that is often favored by women who value consensus over hierarchy.

We also have a preferred social or communication style. There are many different models for categorizing these styles, and I prefer the one developed by Dr. David Merrill back in the 1960s because it is simple to understand and easy to apply. He identified four basic styles:

- *The driver.* Someone who likes you to get to the point quickly and doesn't want to hear all the details.
- *The expressive.* Someone who wants to be noticed and likes to think out loud to generate new ideas.
- *The amiable.* Someone who wants to get along and really cares about the feelings of the entire team.
- *The analytical.* Someone who wants to get it right, wants all the facts before making a decision, and asks lots of questions.

This information can be useful in several ways. First, it's important for you to know your own preferred style because that's the way you communicate naturally. For people who share your preference, it probably works brilliantly. But it might not be as effective for others, so it's important for you to be able to read both the situation and the individual to determine what communication style will have the greatest impact and then be able to adapt your style accordingly.

You can usually identify a person's communication style preference by watching how that person communicates with others. And if you can determine that person's preferred style, you can figure out how to speak to him to best get your point across to him. While most people communicate with others the way they like others to communicate with them, it actually is much more effective if you adapt your style to what works best for the other person. So, if you are talking with someone who is analytical, be sure to have plenty of facts and figures to back up your point, and be logical in your approach. But if you are speaking to a driver, get right to the bottom line and let that person ask you questions in order to fill in the details that matter.

Hillary is known for doing this very well. Both Richard Holbrooke and George Mitchell, who worked with her extensively in 2009, said that she has been helpful in bluntly assessing the personalities of the people she deals with, which enables her to adapt her style when communicating with them. In an article for the *Washington Post* by Glenn Kessler, Mitchell said: "One of the reasons she is so effective is because she is so direct. She is able to state in simple terms complicated issues." During a recent controversy over Hillary's exchange with Pakistani businessmen and students, Paul Richter of the *Los Angeles Times* wrote, "Clinton has earned a reputation for sometimes speaking with candor more closely associated with senators than chief diplomats." The Associated Press agreed with this assessment:

"As a political spouse, career public official and recently as a diplomat, Clinton has long showed a tendency toward bluntness." This follows my golden rule: Do unto others as they want to be done unto. And this is what I mean when I say that you need to be able to adapt your communication style to the person as well as the situation.

Second, another aspect of adapting your style is realizing that if you have a very strong preference for a particular style, you might not be aware of all the perceptions you are inadvertently creating. For example, if you are extremely analytical, you might seem to be very thorough and accurate but also rigid and inflexible. If you are a very strong driver, you may seem great at multitasking and getting things done quickly but also insensitive to the feelings of others or too quick to make decisions. And so on. So, it's important to get feedback from those you trust on how you are being perceived and then adapt your communication style to leverage your strengths and mitigate your weaknesses. After all, most of the time, perception is considered reality, and you can affect those perceptions by being intentional about what and how you communicate.

Finally, you can be more effective as a leader if you know how to adapt your communication style effectively when you are trying to influence others. My company does a program on effective influencing that covers four ways in which people make decisions. I'll briefly explain the four ways so that you get an idea of what I mean. Here they are:

- *Dominance.* Realistic, pragmatic, independent, needs facts to decide, prefers efficient alternatives
- *Intuition.* Venturesome, likes to involve others, willing to take risks, prefers creative and fresh ideas
- *Steadiness.* Weighs options, idealistic, tentative, concerned about the impact on others, prefers group consensus
- *Conscientiousness.* Logical—step-by-step, conservative, slow to decide, likes to study all the alternatives, prefers proven alternatives

You can probably guess which decision-making approach goes with each of the social/communication styles. The direct style uses the dominance approach, the expressive style uses the intuitive approach, the amiable style uses the steadiness approach, and the analytical style uses the conscientious approach.

If you can identify a person's preferred social style, you can figure out how she is most likely to make a decision and communicate with her in a way that makes it easier for her to decide in your favor. You can also sense how to engage in a conversation that will be most satisfying to that person, such as whether you should stress the logical, emotional, or cooperative aspects of the situation.

The only other point I want to make about adapting your style is to remember to do this within your comfort zone. If you try to adapt in a way that is not authentic for you, it will be very difficult. Also, you should flex this muscle slowly so that you can learn what works best for you as you go along. Just being aware of this need to adapt will move you in a better direction and cause you to be more sensitive to the needs of the other person, which is what being a resilient leader is all about.

✛ SECRET 4: LISTEN WITH INTENTION ✛

I can't understand why listening isn't taught in elementary school, high school, college, and even graduate school. The reason can't be that the skill isn't critical—we all know that it is. Nor can it be that we do it so well intuitively—because we don't. Nor that we don't know how to break listening down into teachable elements—because we do. Maybe the academic world thinks that we will learn it by osmosis. And we probably won't.

Yet listening is one of the most essential skills that we use in awesome communication. In addition to understanding the meaning of the words that are spoken, listening involves such things as reading nonverbal messages, discerning the emotional implications that are carried in the tone of the voice, interpreting what is *not* being said and why, and surmising meaning from the context of the situation. The list is long, and here is something that might surprise you: I saw a study once that reported that *tone* was responsible for 38 percent of our communication effectiveness, and *words* were responsible for only 7 percent! As you can see, listening is a pretty complex skill.

When I say that as a leader, it's important for you to listen to learn, I'm really talking about listening with the intention of better understanding someone or something. In order to do this, you have to practice active listening. Hearing what someone says isn't enough. You need to be constantly discerning two key things: meaning and feelings. What is this person *really* saying, and how is she *really* feeling about it?

To do this, you must be able to suspend your judgment while you are listening and replace it with curiosity. You need to be asking yourself the "w" questions—who, what, where, when, and why—in order to truly understand. For example: Who all are involved? What is really happening here? Where are we being affected? When does this occur? Why is this important? And finally, you need to be asking: So what? What are the implications? What can we do about it?

Hillary does this extraordinarily well. Her colleague Kristin Mannion shared with me that when Hillary is listening to someone, she focuses totally on that person and spends a great deal of time questioning him in order to truly understand what he is saying so that she can make an informed decision or advance the mission that she is working on. She listens with intention. Kristin said, "She earnestly wants to learn as a listener. And, you can disagree with her and it is okay, but she will always want to know *why*. She wants to understand your point of view and be able to relate to your perspective in a real rather than a superficial way." I think that's an important trait of resilient leaders.

You also need to check your understanding as you are listening. We all have different filters through which we determine the meaning of what we are hearing, so it's important to check that what you "heard" is what the person actually said. An easy way to do this is to paraphrase or summarize back to the person what you think she meant and have her validate that you are getting it right or correct you where you may have misunderstood her. An example of this is: "Are you saying that . . . ?" or, "I think I heard you mention three things that you feel are critical. They are . . . Did I miss anything?" This not only ensures that you are getting it right, but also lets the other person know how important it is to you that you understand what she is saying. And when the other person thinks that you care enough to really understand her, she is more likely to try to understand you in return.

Here are a few more tips for listening with intention:

- Avoid thinking about what you are going to say in response while someone is talking to you. I know this is hard to do, because that little voice in our head just keeps babbling away, but you can turn it down for a while if you are aware that it is keeping you from listening with intention.

- Be patient and avoid interrupting. Let the person complete his thought before you respond. Remember to "bite your tongue," as my mother would always tell me.
- Watch the nonverbals and know that if they are not matching the verbals, there is probably a disconnect between what the person is saying and what she really thinks or feels.
- Listen with empathy. It's important that you be able to feel both the joy and the pain.

⊹ SECRET 5: DON'T AVOID ⊹ THE HARD CONVERSATIONS

I once heard that the definition of a difficult conversation is anything that's hard to talk about. Some things come to my mind immediately: a performance review with someone who is performing poorly, a neighbor's dog who barks constantly at 2 a.m., or the decision that your boss made that you feel is totally wrong. There are many conversations like these that we avoid, either because we fear the response and repercussions or because we are afraid that we will make someone feel bad. Most leaders I know would rather tackle more hard work or solve more impossible problems than have these conversations. However, resilient leaders must have them. And, in the process, they must have the courage to speak the truth.

Now, I know that this is easier to say than to do, since what stops us is not our ability, but our fears. So, let's look at what you can do to minimize the fear and encourage yourself to initiate a hard conversation. First, do your homework. Learn as much as you can about the situation. Check the facts, and don't rely on someone's opinion. Try to get a variety of perspectives. And be clear with yourself about what you really want the result of the conversation to be. Hillary is known for doing this, as I mentioned in Chapter 3. She is naturally curious and has learned to be well prepared.

But, also recognize that what you learn about the situation is only your side of the story. In the difficult conversation, you want to learn the other person's side of the story as well, because the truth probably resides in a combination of both stories. Your active listening skills will help you to do this.

Second, do your best to suspend your judgment. When you approach someone and you are in the mindset of right/wrong, good/bad, or should/shouldn't, you will inadvertently transmit a threat to that person, and he will naturally become defensive. That's just how it works. So, as I've said before, replace this judgment mindset with curiosity, and you will be less likely to get the "fight-or-flight" response from the other person. As a result, the issue will be easier for both of you to discuss.

And finally, it is better to have conversations of this kind sooner rather than later. I can't tell you how many times I've coached a leader who has to deliver a tough message to someone, and it's very clear that if she had addressed the issue with the person when it first surfaced, discussing it would have been much easier for both of them. Most of the time, the longer you wait, the more emotional the conversation will be. And the irony is that when you do have these conversations, and they are done skillfully with good intentions, they often lift the tension, reduce the stress, and create greater mutual respect and trust between you and the individual.

I think Hillary knew that in her role as secretary of state, she would need the members of her team to be able to have these difficult conversations with her and with one another. In one of her early talks to the employees in the State Department, she encouraged people to speak up and share their views honestly. She said, "I want you to give me the best advice you can. I want you to understand there is nothing that I welcome more than a good debate and the kind of dialogue that will make us better." She later closed that meeting by saying, "So . . . we need to have a sense of openness and candor in this building. And I invite that. Now, not everyone's ideas will make it into policy, but we will be better because we have heard from you." If you can establish this same kind of candor with your team, you will be laying the foundation for having difficult conversations that are part of the awesome communication of resilient leaders.

Here's a quick self-assessment for awesome communication:

- Do you communicate what the future can look like in a way that causes employees to want to give their discretionary effort to be successful?
- Are you communicating in a positive way that conveys a "can do" attitude?
- Are you able to speak from your heart and be emotionally expressive when you want others to connect with you and your message?
- Do you empathize with others and convey that empathy in your words and actions?
- Do you know your own preferred social/communication style, and can you adapt it to deal more effectively with others?
- Do you actively listen to others by suspending judgment and being curious?
- Do you check your assumptions about what someone is saying to you?
- Do you take the initiative to have conversations that you feel might be uncomfortable?
- Do you encourage your team members to be respectfully open and honest with you and with one another?
- Are you making your words count in a way that helps others be more resilient in times of great challenges and significant change?

Again, here are the five secrets for awesome communication.

SECRETS FOR AWESOME COMMUNICATION

Secret 1: Inspire action.

Secret 2: Speak from your heart.

Secret 3: Adapt your style.

Secret 4: Listen with intention.

Secret 5: Don't avoid the hard conversations.

CHAPTER 8

LEADING WITH PURPOSE

I know that you've thought about purpose in terms of a project at work or the reason for holding a meeting, but have you really thought about the *purpose* of your life? It's a very interesting thing to do. However, it's not easy. We are so busy getting through our day-to-day activities that few of us have time to consider anything much past the next hour or the next day. But, if you think about your life as a journey, don't you want to know what your destination is? Wouldn't knowing this make the trip more interesting? Wouldn't it help you choose the best route, help you get over the bumps in the road along the way, and possibly even keep you going when you get tired or frustrated or disappointed?

For each of us, our purpose in life, simply stated, is our reason for being. It usually has something to do with concern for the "greater good"—achieving something for the benefit of others. When we are starting our career, this sense of purpose is often overshadowed by the drive to satisfy our basic needs for food, clothing, and shelter. Then we move on to the need to belong to a group and achieve success within an organization. But, often, even during these times when we are focused on specific pursuits, we are also driven to make a difference. Some people want to save the environment, some want to help the disabled, while others want to help those who are less fortunate. And this sense of purpose is not static.

At different points in your life, different things can be important to you. If you have children, they can become the focus of your time and energy for many years. However, I encourage you to think beyond your immediate family when you are considering what is truly significant to you and where you want to create your legacy.

As far as I know, we aren't born with this sense of purpose. Either we are taught it as a fundamental value, or we have an experience that strikes a chord within us that resonates so deeply that we can't shake it. This happened to Hillary.

In her younger years, she often went with friends from her Sunday school class to visit the migrant workers in her community. She realized early in her life how difficult the conditions were for the young children of these hard-working families. They lacked proper health care and education, and yet they all had a sense of hope in their lives. This was just one of many experiences that inspired Hillary and gave her life a sense of purpose.

Over the course of many years, Hillary dedicated her time and energy to creating better living conditions for young children. She eventually served on the boards of the Arkansas Children's Hospital Legal Services and the Children's Defense Fund, and she published a scholarly article in the *Yale Law Journal* called "Children's Policies: Abandonment and Neglect" in 1977. The article explored the difficult decisions that the judiciary and society face when children are abused or neglected by their families, decisions that can have such consequences as denying a child medical care or the right to remain in school. Also in 1977, she cofounded the Arkansas Advocates for Children and Families, a statewide alliance with the Children's Defense Fund that investigated the conditions under which juveniles were incarcerated in adult jails. The alliance ulimately led an effort to separate juveniles from the general population in order to provide them with more protection and faster adjudication. And, of course, throughout the rest of her political life, children were often at the heart of her initiatives. All of this started as a result of Hillary's being exposed early in her life to experiences that inspired her to serve children—not for money or for fame, but because it was something that she deeply cared about.

Living a purposeful life can also be a unique source of energy. Candy Crowley, a well-known CNN reporter who has followed Hillary for years and was close to her throughout the presidential campaign, said that you can't have the kind of energy and focus that Hillary has without having a strong sense of purpose. In other words, Candy said, "You keep going if you believe in something." This strong sense of purpose, as outlined in Hillary's political platform, helped her stay focused and on task during the toughest times in the campaign. When people said that she might not win the Democratic presidential nomination, she worked that much harder. Candy went on to say that it requires a lot of energy to run a national campaign. Just the sheer travel and having to "be on all the time" is too stressful for many candidates. She shared with me about a time when she was covering the campaign and Hillary flew out to the West Coast for a rally and then flew back to the East Coast on the red-eye to be interviewed on one of the major talk shows the next morning at 7 a.m. If you have ever taken a red-eye, you know that it means that you get practically no sleep that night. Candy said, "She loves talking about policy issues and believes that this is one area where she can have an impact and help to change things for the better." Hillary is living with purpose in her life.

On a side note, according to two recent studies, Hillary may live a better life and live longer as a result of her having purpose in her life! In a study conducted by the University of Rochester's Human Motivation Research Group, people who lived with purpose exhibited more interest, excitement, and confidence—as well as greater persistence, creativity, and performance—than a control group who were motivated largely by external demands and rewards. And according to a study done by the Rush University Medical Center, people who had a higher sense of purpose were more likely to live longer than those who did not.

If we are clear about our sense of purpose, we can often translate it into our work life and gain greater fulfillment from our work experience. For example, I'm passionate about helping to further the advancement of great leaders. That's what I really get excited about doing. As a result, I serve on the board of an organization that promotes the leadership potential of women who are reentering the workforce. And I've been fortunate enough to build a business that focuses on leadership development in Fortune 500 companies.

You can also translate your passion into your role as a leader. Let me explain what I mean by this. Here are two common areas where a business leader's sense of *purpose* might be aligned with what he does every day:

Purpose	*Work*
• To be of service to others	• Coaching and mentoring employees
	• Training new employees
	• Leading a team through change
• To improve things	• Doing research and development for causes that are important to you; getting involved
	• Starting up new ventures
	• Leading transformation efforts inside or outside your organization

So, are you living with purpose? And is it influencing your work? Here are four questions to help you decide:

- Do you often find yourself immersed in something that you are working on, so that the time seems to just fly by?
- Are you excited when you get up to go to work every day? Do you look forward to getting there and getting started on what you plan to do that day?
- Do you have something you are working toward that makes you feel that you are making a difference?

- Can you imagine getting through difficult times and facing serious obstacles because what you are doing is worth the agony and effort?

If you answered yes to these questions, you are probably doing something at work that is aligned with your values and your purpose in life. And this alignment is a great source of your resilience. Here are five secrets for capitalizing on the purpose in your life.

⊹ SECRET 1: IDENTIFY YOUR ⊹ PURPOSE IN LIFE

What do you believe in so strongly that you are willing to give your discretionary effort to make it happen? Life presents us with an opportunity to serve and, in return, to gain a sense of fulfillment like no other. I call this your *purpose* in life.

What is your purpose? What could be so important to you that you would be willing to take on a job where you must try to stop Iran's nuclear program, curb Pakistan's Islamic insurgency, and help new U.S. forces in Afghanistan with civilian projects? What could make it okay for you to go to very dangerous places and address crowds that are skeptical of everything you have to say? What could keep you up at night reading briefing after briefing in order to understand the issues and be prepared to represent your country in a dialogue? We know what matters enough to Hillary to have her doing these things in her role as secretary of state: She needs to clearly understand the issue or situation she is dealing with so as to choose the course of action that will have the right kind of impact—the "right" approach or change. The real question is, what matters that much to you?

Maybe you already know the answer to my question. A friend and colleague of mine knows her purpose in life. She has a son with severe learning disabilities. As a result, she became committed to making a difference for people who are suffering in life through no fault of their own. She started a Washington, D.C., chapter of the Achilles Track Club (for physically disabled athletes), organized a soup kitchen in suburban Maryland, and coordinated volunteers for an orphanage in a major city. At work, she runs the United Way campaign for a Fortune 500 company, where she is in charge of major change management efforts that affect large groups in the organization. The single thread that ties all of these activities together is her desire to help other people who happen to be having a hard time—for whatever reason. Needless to say, she is a very busy woman. But she never seems to run out of energy, and she is one of the most positive people I know. She understands what matters to her and why. It's important for you to know that about yourself.

Here are some questions to consider:

- What are you really looking for in your work? Are you looking for more money, recognition, or power? Or are you being intentional about focusing on things that bring you the greatest personal satisfaction and truly make a difference for others?

- Whom do you know who seems to have this higher sense of purpose? How is it reflected in this person's day-to-day activities and behaviors? What is that purpose, and why is this person committed to it? How does it affect others? What effect does this person have on you?

- Think about a time in the past when you exercised leadership and pushed beyond your comfort zone and/or you stayed focused as a result of your determination and internal drive. What brought you a sense of fulfillment, joy, and energy? Does this situation suggest an area that you care deeply about? What might that be?

- Where and how would you like to make a difference? How would you feel if you never made any progress in that area? If your perceived level of regret is high enough, this might indicate a purpose for you at this stage in your life.

If you are leading a team or organization, you can also create a sense of purpose around you. Together with your team, generate a list of reasons why people are focused on what they are doing. Involve people by having them share their thoughts and feelings about the positive outcomes of their efforts. Then have them prioritize the list and come up with a shared meaning of what success would look like based on the purposes that have been identified. Having a sense of purpose within your organization or team is key to maintaining both commitment and focus. It keeps people engaged in their day-to-day work. It also serves as a compass when the team is getting off track in a meeting, a strategy session, or its daily activities.

✠ SECRET 2: MOVE YOUR ✠ PURPOSE FORWARD

Some people who are clear about their purpose in life have a problem with taking action in order to realize it. It's all about being focused and intentional. In his book *A Woman in Charge,* Carl Bernstein states, "As a girl and then as a women, Hillary has almost always been desperate to be a passionate participant and at the center of events: familial, generational, experiential, political, historical. Call it ambition, call it the desire to make the world a better place—she has been driven. Rarely has she stepped aside voluntarily into passivity."

Bernstein goes on to say, "Three pillars have held her up through one crisis after another in a life creased by personal difficulties and public and private battles: her religious faith; her powerful urge toward both service and its accompanying sense (for good or ill) of self-importance; and a fierce desire for privacy." This urge *to be of service* gave her a sense of direction and a road map for the actions she has taken throughout her personal and professional endeavors.

Remember that the return from realizing and actualizing your purpose is a greater sense of energy and feeling of fulfillment in the total context of your life. It's an anchor to help bring you back when you get off track, and it generates the desire to continue when you feel stuck or even defeated.

Here are some tips to consider for actualizing your purpose:

- Ask yourself what stands in the way of your taking some kind of action toward realizing your purpose. People often tell me that they just don't have enough time to do everything they want to do. Take a look at your daily activities and ask yourself which areas bring value to your whole life and which don't. Ask yourself which tasks you can eliminate or change, or even delegate, in order to gain more time to focus on your purpose.

- Do some research. Take time to talk with other people who live a purposeful life. Ask them what motivates them to do the purposeful things they do. Then ask them how they maintain their purpose, particularly during times of change, excessive stress, conflicting expectations from others, and so on.

- Identify an area that gives you tremendous energy and fulfillment. Ask yourself where your natural passions lie when you are making contributions to this area. What personal and professional strengths have you blended in these experiences? What can you do now to leverage those same strengths to forward your purpose?

- Begin to formulate your "purpose" statement. Say it out loud to yourself until describing it becomes natural, and then share it with close friends and colleagues. Here are a few examples to help you get started:
  - "To be a positive and supportive teacher of young children."
  - "To be a change agent for my organization in order to enable the people and the organization to get through these hard times successfully."
  - "To be of service to my community by addressing the needs and challenges of people who are less fortunate than I."
  - "To be the most caring, supportive, and helpful friend, colleague, parent, or spouse that I can be."

SECRET 3: KEEP YOUR PURPOSE ALIVE

It's easy to lose your sense of purpose in the frenzy of every-day life, so you need to "check in" with yourself once in a while to be sure that you are staying focused on what's really important to you. When I am feeling overwhelmed by the day-to-day activities of running a company and I begin to feel drained, the best thing I can do is speak at a conference or some sort of leadership forum. That always seems to get me back on track and feeling fulfilled again.

Recently, I took a red-eye flight back from the West Coast to speak at a Latino conference. A few short hours after landing in Washington, D.C., I spent 90 minutes leading a large group of emerging leaders through a process to expand their awareness of their leadership potential, then gave them some tools and techniques for leading projects back in their work environments. At the end of the session, I felt totally energized, and I could have continued with the group for hours without feeling tired or losing interest. Knowing that I might be making a difference to these potential leaders is what keeps me going, no matter what my calendar looks like or what issues I may be addressing back in the office. Experiences like this remind me of what I am all about and keep me on track when I am tempted to spend too much of my time being an executive. And I think this happens to many of us who take on a major leadership role in an organization. We get away from doing what we love to do on a daily basis, so we need to find intentional ways to keep our sense of purpose alive.

You can do this by integrating certain reminders, experiences, and rituals into your life. These could be such things as

- Speaking at events on a topic that you care about— that forwards your purpose

- Mentoring a colleague or a friend
- Participating in a community program such as a soup kitchen
- Teaching as a volunteer
- Reaching out to make a difference in the efforts made by your church, your children's school, a professional association, or some other such institution
- Reading an inspirational book on something that you are passionate about
- Keeping an inspiring saying on your computer, at your desk, or even on the refrigerator

To keep purpose alive in your organizations, consider having staff meetings or retreats where people can join in discussions concerning the company's values and principles. It is also helpful to engage the company's leaders and managers in the orientation programs for new employees, so that they can speak about the values, credos, and mission of the organization. While it is good for new employees to know this information, it's equally beneficial for existing staff members to be reminded of it.

SECRET 4: BLEND YOUR AMBITIONS WITH YOUR ASPIRATIONS

One of the greatest gifts in life is to be able to take your dreams and blend them into your ambitions. Let me explain. I have always been interested in helping women get ahead in business. I started my career in a male-dominated industry—as a supervisor of men working on a production line. I had no female mentors or managers who could help me learn how to survive in a male-dominated business environment. I had to learn it by myself, and at times the lessons were very painful. As a result, I have always tried to help other women—as I would have appreciated having a woman help me. I started by helping women create networks so that they could connect with others and create a sense of community for mutual support on the issues and challenges that they faced at work. I coached women on how to be more politically savvy and how to have greater influence with key decision makers in their organizations. Then, when I started my own business, which focuses on leadership development, I had the idea of designing a leadership development program that was focused on the unique needs and gifts of women who were aspiring to be leaders. I started the Women in Leadership and Learning program, which was, at that time, the first course of its kind in the United States. It is still in demand today, and it is actually the flagship program of an entire division of my company. I was able to blend my passion for helping women advance in their careers with my business goal of growing a successful business.

You can also blend your sense of purpose with your everyday activities by simply retaining your focus and behaving with specific intention. Remember that taking action on your purpose does not have to be something monumental. It is just being conscious of your purpose and being open to the opportunities around you on a daily basis. I spoke recently with Denise Christy, president of Humana Michigan, and we were talking about the strong connection between purpose and resilience. In many ways, Denise seems to have a natural "flow" in her life. She has very little internal conflict and seems always to be focused on her purpose. Denise's purpose in life is finding ways to help others and the community. She makes every day purposeful. She is always aware and intentional about bringing value to a conversation or taking appropriate action when dealing with a difficult or opportunistic situation. In addition to working to find better ways for men and women to be successful in her company as part of her leadership role there, she also does this outside of her formal duties.

Denise said, "Every time I have a lunch meeting, I want it to be a helpful experience for someone. When I walk into that restaurant, I want to make sure our time together is not just an opportunity for catching up, but that we engage in purposeful conversation. It might be that I can help someone to see something in himself that no one has shared with him before, or it might be that we have a brainstorming session about an issue that is important to that person. I never know exactly what the lunch conversation will look like, but my focus is always, how can I help you?"

Denise said that it is important for her to be able to look back at her life many years from now and see that she has had an impact on the quality of people's lives. Then she will know that she has made a difference.

So, think about your purpose in life and look for opportunities, both large and small, to blend it into your work experiences as well as your personal interactions.

⊹ SECRET 5: START NOW! ⊹

One of the major shifts in our world today is knowing that it's all about making a choice now. It's not about waiting for someone to bring you an instruction book for how to live a successful life. It's about leading from within and taking the responsibility for shaping your life the way you want it to be. This takes hard work, strong commitment, a great deal of energy, and a strong sense of purpose. Each day that you don't live on purpose is a day that is lost to you and perhaps to others. We are living in a world that is striving to rebuild itself and find a greater level of continuity and stability. We aren't there yet, and it might take a while. But I am very sure that the people who will lead us to that better place are those who live and lead out of a sense of purpose.

Remember that the bigger the storm, the more likely we are to revert to our old habits or lose our energy to forge ahead with innovative solutions to new challenges. People who have a strong sense of purpose, whatever that means to them, will weather the storm, and they will naturally guide themselves and their teams to a place where they can best align with the conditions of the day, meaning that they will find the "goodness" of what they can bring to any situation, and they will act on it. This is what being a resilient leader is all about.

So what's stopping you from living and leading with purpose? Here are some final suggestions to help you get started:

- Take care of yourself. Surround yourself with people and situations that give you energy and inspire you to move beyond the day-to-day routine of life in order to focus on a higher calling.
- Think more broadly and deeply. Identifying and realizing a sense of purpose means stepping back and checking in on the four main quadrants of your life: the physical, emotional, mental, and spiritual. When these are in harmony, you will find a flow, and the doors of opportunity will start to open. What are you doing to enrich these four quadrants on a day-to-day basis? If one area is deprived, look for ways to enhance that part of your life. This will help you to stay focused and intentional about your higher level of purpose and the extraordinary role that it can play in your life.
- Finally, we should all ask ourselves these questions: Who do we want to be at the end? What do we want

other people to say about us when we are gone? What do we want our legacy to be?

Lead on!

SECRETS FOR LIVING YOUR LIFE WITH PURPOSE

Secret 1: Identify your purpose in life.

Secret 2: Move your purpose forward.

Secret 3: Keep your purpose alive.

Secret 4: Blend your ambitions with your aspirations.

Secret 5: Start now!

CHAPTER 9

FINAL THOUGHTS

The World Is Changing—

Are You?

There are many changes and major shifts going on in our world, country, and organizations today. The complexities in our environment are causing business leaders to question what the future will hold, what the "new normal" will actually look like. It's my belief that we are not there yet and that it will be some time before we are able to determine that new equilibrium. Regardless of whether you are at the top of your organization, leading a team, or volunteering in your community, you are sure to be challenged and to experience difficult circumstances. It's just a fact of life. And when this happens, you will have a choice whether to avoid those difficult situations or face them head-on. Resilient leaders will do the latter and will consider these challenges as opportunities to develop a greater level of wisdom, competence, and inner confidence. Remember that what makes "great" leaders is not only their successes but also their approach to adapting to change and to handling misfortune or even failure.

As my dear father, Max Shambaugh, has always said, "Life is just one big adventure—filled with ups and downs, but ultimately just what we make of it." The essence of this book reinforces my father's perspective that we have more control over our success and happiness than we might think we do. The control of our destiny starts with our self-knowledge, core beliefs, and pervasive mindsets. These affect our confidence, motivation, and perseverance, qualities that are tied directly to our ability to be resilient in challenging times. Each of us has the capacity to reach our highest level of achievement regardless of the inevitable obstacles and challenges that life presents. It's all about the choices we make on a daily basis.

⊹ IT'S ABOUT CHOICE ⊹

The good news is that organizations are shifting from managers who support the hierarchal "command and control" work climate to leaders who encourage more engagement, choice, and personal accountability. This means we all have the power and influence to realize professional success, regardless of how we define that for ourselves. It also means that no one is going to hand us an instruction book to deal with change, misfortune, or failure. We are going to have to figure that out for ourselves, just as Hillary Clinton did. Hillary's extraordinary success was largely due to her ability to live and lead within the *Secrets of Being Resilient*. As this book illustrates, she had many disappointments, setbacks, and changes in her life. What helped her to get through to "the other side of the storm" was her true endurance and resilience. We can learn so very much from her. As you continue to build your self-awareness, I hope you will use the insights in this book to tap into her *6 Leadership Secrets* of Being Resilient, Being a Continuous Learner, Being Authentic, Embracing Change, Being Connected, and Leading with Purpose in order to make great choices for yourself and others.

✝ BELIEVE! ✝

Remember, resilience is not running a marathon and crossing the finish line, but rather, it's tapping into your inner core and knowing that you can do it! I remember that in 2008 Macy's had "Believe" on the side of its holiday shopping bags. Perhaps that word should be the slogan for becoming a resilient leader. Those who are "great" leaders, and who will successfully persevere through the days ahead, will believe in themselves and create powerful visions that others can also believe in. Obviously, this will require deep thought, careful planning, and intentional action to be successful in the "new normal." So, begin today by determining how these *secrets* can help you to become a resilient leader. And then, be the torch for others to follow your example!

CHAPTER 10

LEADERSHIP
SECRETS
IN ACTION

⊹ DEMOCRATIC NATIONAL CONVENTION ⊹
AUGUST 26, 2008

I am honored to be here tonight. A proud mother. A proud Democrat. A proud American. And a proud supporter of Barack Obama.

My friends, it is time to take back the country we love.

Whether you voted for me, or voted for Barack, the time is now to unite as a single party with a single purpose. We are on the same team, and none of us can sit on the sidelines.

This is a fight for the future. And it's a fight we must win.

I haven't spent the past 35 years in the trenches advocating for children, campaigning for universal health care, helping parents balance work and family, and fighting for women's rights at home and around the world . . . to see another Republican in the White House squander the promise of our country and the hopes of our people.

And you haven't worked so hard over the last 18 months, or endured the last eight years, to suffer through more failed leadership.

No way. No how. No McCain.

Barack Obama is my candidate. And he must be our president.

Tonight we need to remember what a presidential election is really about. When the polls have closed, and the ads are finally off the air, it comes down to you—the American people, your lives, and your children's futures.

For me, it's been a privilege to meet you in your homes, your workplaces, and your communities. Your stories reminded me every day that America's greatness is bound up in the lives of the American people—your hard work, your devotion to duty, your love for your children, and your determination to keep going, often in the face of enormous obstacles.

You taught me so much, you made me laugh, and . . . you even made me cry. You allowed me to become part of your lives. And you became part of mine.

I will always remember the single mom who had adopted two kids with autism, didn't have health insurance, and discovered she had cancer. But she greeted me with her bald head painted with my name on it and asked me to fight for health care.

I will always remember the young man in a Marine Corps T-shirt who waited months for medical care and said to me: "Take care of my buddies; a lot of them are still over there . . . and then will you please help take care of me?"

I will always remember the boy who told me his mom worked for the minimum wage and that her employer had cut her hours. He said he just didn't know what his family was going to do.

I will always be grateful to everyone from all 50 states, Puerto Rico, and the territories, who joined our campaign on behalf of all those people left out and left behind by the Bush administrtation.

To my supporters, my champions—my sisterhood of the traveling pantsuits—from the bottom of my heart: thank you.

You never gave in. You never gave up. And together we made history.

Along the way, America lost two great Democratic champions who would have been here with us tonight. One of our finest young leaders, Arkansas Democratic Party chair, Bill Gwatney, who believed with all his heart that America and the South could be and should be Democratic from top to bottom.

And Congresswoman Stephanie Tubbs Jones, a dear friend to many of us, a loving mother, and courageous leader who never gave up her quest to make America fairer and smarter, stronger, and better. Steadfast in her beliefs, a fighter of uncommon grace, she was an inspiration to me and to us all.

Our heart goes out to Stephanie's son, Mervyn, Jr., and Bill's wife, Rebecca, who traveled to Denver to join us at our convention.

Bill and Stephanie knew that after eight years of George Bush, people are hurting at home, and our standing has eroded around the world. We have a lot of work ahead.

Jobs lost, houses gone, falling wages, rising prices. The Supreme Court in a right-wing headlock and our government in partisan gridlock. The biggest deficit in our nation's history. Money borrowed from the Chinese to buy oil from the Saudis.

Putin and Georgia, Iraq and Iran.

I ran for president to renew the promise of America. To rebuild the middle class and sustain the American Dream, to provide the opportunity to work hard and have that work rewarded, to save for college, a home and retirement, to afford the gas and groceries and still have a little left over each month.

To promote a clean energy economy that will create millions of green collar jobs.

To create a health care system that is universal, high quality, and affordable so that parents no longer have to choose between care for themselves or their children or be stuck in dead-end jobs simply to keep their insurance.

To create a world-class education system and make college affordable again.

To fight for an America defined by deep and meaningful equality—from civil rights to labor rights, from women's rights to gay rights, from ending discrimination to promoting unionization to providing help for the most important job there is: caring for our families. To help every child live up to his or her God-given potential.

To make America once again a nation of immigrants and a nation of laws.

To bring fiscal sanity back to Washington and make our government an instrument of the public good, not of private plunder.

To restore America's standing in the world, to end the war in Iraq, bring our troops home, and honor their service by caring for our veterans.

And to join with our allies to confront our shared challenges, from poverty and genocide to terrorism and global warming.

Most of all, I ran to stand up for all those who have been invisible to their government for eight long years.

Those are the reasons I ran for president. Those are the reasons I support Barack Obama. And those are the reasons you should too.

I want you to ask yourselves: Were you in this campaign just for me? Or were you in it for that young Marine and others like him? Were you in it for that mom struggling with cancer while raising her kids? Were you in it for that boy and his mom surviving on the minimum wage? Were you in it for all the people in this country who feel invisible?

We need leaders once again who can tap into that special blend of American confidence and optimism that has enabled generations before us to meet our toughest challenges. Leaders who can help us show ourselves and the world that with our ingenuity, creativity, and innovative spirit, there are no limits to what is possible in America.

This won't be easy. Progress never is. But it will be impossible if we don't fight to put a Democrat in the White House.

We need to elect Barack Obama because we need a president who understands that America can't compete in a global economy by padding the pockets of energy speculators, while ignoring the workers whose jobs have been shipped overseas. We need a president who understands that we can't solve the problems of global warming by giving windfall profits to the oil companies while ignoring opportunities to invest in new technologies that will build a green economy.

We need a president who understands that the genius of America has always depended on the strength and vitality of the middle class.

Barack Obama began his career fighting for workers displaced by the global economy. He built his campaign on a fundamental belief that change in this country must start from the ground up, not the top down. He knows government must be about "We the people" not "We the favored few."

And when Barack Obama is in the White House, he'll revitalize our economy, defend the working people of America, and meet the global challenges of our time. Democrats know how to do this. As I recall, President Clinton and the Democrats did it before. And President Obama and the Democrats will do it again.

He'll transform our energy agenda by creating millions of green jobs and building a new, clean energy future. He'll make sure that middle class families get the tax relief they deserve. And I can't wait to watch Barack Obama sign a health care plan into law that covers every single American.

Barack Obama will end the war in Iraq responsibly and bring our troops home—a first step to repairing our alliances around the world.

And he will have with him a terrific partner in Michelle Obama. Anyone who saw Michelle's speech last night knows she will be a great First Lady for America.

Americans are also fortunate that Joe Biden will be at Barack Obama's side. He is a strong leader and a good man. He understands both the economic stresses here at home and the strategic challenges abroad. He is pragmatic, tough, and wise. And, of course, Joe will be supported by his wonderful wife, Jill.

They will be a great team for our country.

Now, John McCain is my colleague and my friend.

He has served our country with honor and courage.

But we don't need four more years . . . of the last eight years.

More economic stagnation . . . and less affordable health care.

More high gas prices . . . and less alternative energy.

More jobs getting shipped overseas . . . and fewer jobs created here.

More skyrocketing debt . . . home foreclosures . . . and mounting bills that are crushing our middle class families.

More war . . . less diplomacy.

More of a government where the privileged come first . . . and everyone else comes last.

John McCain says the economy is fundamentally sound. John McCain doesn't think that 47 million people without health insurance is a crisis. John McCain wants to privatize Social Security. And in 2008, he still thinks it's okay when women don't earn equal pay for equal work.

With an agenda like that, it makes sense that George Bush and John McCain will be together next week in the Twin Cities. Because these days they're awfully hard to tell apart.

America is still around after 232 years because we have risen to the challenge of every new time, changing to be faithful to our values of equal opportunity for all and the common good.

And I know what that can mean for every man, woman, and child in America. I'm a United States Senator because in 1848 a group of courageous women and a few brave men gathered in Seneca Falls, New York, many traveling for days and nights, to participate in the first convention on women's rights in our history.

And so dawned a struggle for the right to vote that would last 72 years, handed down by mother to daughter to granddaughter—and a few sons and grandsons along the way.

These women and men looked into their daughters' eyes, imagined a fairer and freer world, and found the strength to fight. To rally and picket. To endure ridicule and harassment. To brave violence and jail.

And after so many decades—88 years ago on this very day—the nineteenth amendment guaranteeing women the right to vote would be forever enshrined in our Constitution.

My mother was born before women could vote. But in this election my daughter got to vote for her mother for president.

This is the story of America. Of women and men who defy the odds and never give up.

How do we give this country back to them?

By following the example of a brave New Yorker, a woman who risked her life to shepherd slaves along the Underground Railroad.

And on that path to freedom, Harriett Tubman had one piece of advice.

If you hear the dogs, keep going.

If you see the torches in the woods, keep going.

If they're shouting after you, keep going.

Don't ever stop. Keep going.

If you want a taste of freedom, keep going.

Even in the darkest of moments, ordinary Americans have found the faith to keep going.

I've seen it in you. I've seen it in our teachers and firefighters, nurses and police officers, small business owners and union workers, the men and women of our military—you always keep going.

We are Americans. We're not big on quitting.

But remember, before we can keep going, we have to get going by electing Barack Obama president.

We don't have a moment to lose or a vote to spare.

Nothing less than the fate of our nation and the future of our children hang in the balance.

I want you to think about your children and grandchildren come election day. And think about the choices your parents and grandparents made that had such a big impact on your life and on the life of our nation.

We've got to ensure that the choice we make in this election honors the sacrifices of all who came before us, and will fill the lives of our children with possibility and hope.

That is our duty, to build that bright future, and to teach our children that in America there is no chasm too deep, no barrier too great—and no ceiling too high—for all who work hard, never back down, always keep going, have faith in God, in our country, and in each other.

Thank you so much. God bless America and Godspeed to you all.

⸸ SENATE FOREIGN RELATIONS COMMITTEE ⸸ JANUARY 13, 2009

Thank you, Senator Schumer, for your generous introduction, and even more for your support and our partnership over so many years. You are a valued and trusted colleague, a friend, and a tribute to the people of New York whom you have served with such distinction throughout your career. Mr. Chairman, I offer my congratulations as you take on this new role. You certainly have traveled quite a distance from that day in 1971 when you testified here as a young Vietnam veteran. You have never faltered in your care and concern for our nation, its foreign policy, or its future, and America is in good hands with you leading this committee.

Senator Lugar, I look forward to working with you on a wide range of issues, especially those of greatest concern to you, including the Nunn-Lugar initiative.

And Senator Voinovich, I want to commend you for your service to the people of Ohio and ask for your help in the next two years on the management issues you champion.

It is an honor and a privilege to be here this morning as President-elect Obama's nominee for secretary of state. I am deeply grateful for the trust—and keenly aware of the responsibility—that the president-elect has placed in me to serve our country and our people at a time of such grave dangers, and great possibilities. If confirmed, I will accept the duties of the office with gratitude, humility, and firm determination to represent the United States as energetically and faithfully as I can.

At the same time I must confess that sitting across the table from so many colleagues brings me sadness too. I love the Senate. And if you confirm me for this new role, it will be hard to say good-bye to so many members, Republicans and Democrats, whom I have come to know, admire, and respect deeply, and to the institution where I have been so proud to serve on behalf of the people of New York for the past eight years.

But I assure you that I will be in frequent consultation and conversation with the members of this committee, with the House Foreign Affairs Committee, the appropriations committees, and with Congress as a whole. And I look forward to working with my good friend, Vice President–elect Biden, who has been a valued colleague in the Senate and valued chairman of this committee.

For me, consultation is not a catch-word. It is a commitment. The president-elect and I believe that we must return to the time-honored principle of bipartisanship in our foreign policy—an approach that past presidents of both parties, as well as members of this committee, have subscribed to and that has served our nation well. I look forward to working with all of you to renew America's leadership through diplomacy that enhances our security, advances our interests, and reflects our values. Today, nine years into a new century, Americans know that our nation and our world face great perils: from ongoing wars in Iraq and Afghanistan, to the continuing threat posed by terrorist extremists, to the spread of weapons of mass destruction; from the dangers of climate change to pandemic disease; from financial meltdown to worldwide poverty.

The seventy days since the presidential election offer fresh evidence of the urgency of these challenges. New conflict in Gaza; terrorist attacks in Mumbai; mass killings and rapes in the Congo; cholera in Zimbabwe; reports of record high greenhouse gasses and rapidly melting glaciers; and even an ancient form of terror—piracy—asserting itself in modern form off the Horn of Africa.

Always, and especially in the crucible of these global challenges, our overriding duty is to protect and advance America's security, interests, and values: First, we must keep our people, our nation, and our allies secure. Second, we must promote economic growth and shared prosperity at home and abroad. Finally, we must strengthen America's position of global leadership—ensuring that we remain a positive force in the world, whether in working to preserve the health of our planet or expanding dignity and opportunity for people on the margins whose progress and prosperity will add to our own.

Our world has undergone an extraordinary transformation in the last two decades. In 1989, a wall fell and old barriers began to crumble after 40 years of a Cold War that had influenced every aspect of our foreign policy. By 1999, the rise of more democratic and open societies, the expanding reach of world markets, and the explosion of information technology had made "globalization" the word of the day. For most people, it had primarily an economic connotation, but in fact, we were already living in a profoundly interdependent world in which old rules and boundaries no longer held fast—one in which both the promise and the peril of the twenty-first century could not be contained by national borders or vast distances.

Economic growth has lifted more people out of poverty faster than at any time in history, but economic crises can sweep across the globe even more quickly. A coalition of nations stopped ethnic cleansing in the Balkans, but the conflict in the Middle East continues to inflame tensions from Asia to Africa. Non-state actors fight poverty, improve health, and expand education in the poorest parts of the world, while other non-state actors traffic in drugs, children, and women and kill innocent civilians across the globe.

Now, in 2009, the clear lesson of the last twenty years is that we must both combat the threats and seize the opportunities of our interdependence. And to be effective in doing so we must build a world with more partners and fewer adversaries.

America cannot solve the most pressing problems on our own, and the world cannot solve them without America. The best way to advance America's interest in reducing global threats and seizing global opportunities is to design and implement global solutions. This isn't a philosophical point. This is our reality.

The president-elect and I believe that foreign policy must be based on a marriage of principles and pragmatism, not rigid ideology. On facts and evidence, not emotion or prejudice. Our security, our vitality, and our ability to lead in today's world oblige us to recognize the overwhelming fact of our interdependence.

I believe that American leadership has been wanting but is still wanted. We must use what has been called "smart power": the full range of tools at our disposal—diplomatic, economic, military, political, legal, and cultural—picking the right tool, or combination of tools, for each situation. With smart power, diplomacy will be the vanguard of foreign policy. This is not a radical idea. The ancient Roman poet Terence, who was born a slave and rose to become one of the great voices of his time, declared that "in every endeavor, the seemly course for wise men is to try persuasion first." The same truth binds wise women as well.

The president-elect has made it clear that in the Obama administration there will be no doubt about the leading role of diplomacy. One need only look to North Korea, Iran, the Middle East, and the Balkans to appreciate the absolute necessity of tough-minded, intelligent diplomacy—and the failures that result when that kind of diplomatic effort is absent. And one need only consider the assortment of problems we must tackle in 2009—from fighting terrorism to climate change to global financial crises—to understand the importance of cooperative engagement.

I assure you that, if I am confirmed, the State Department will be firing on all cylinders to provide forward-thinking, sustained diplomacy in every part of the world; applying pressure and exerting leverage; cooperating with our military partners and other agencies of government; partnering effectively with NGOs [non-governemental organizations], the private sector, and international organizations; using modern technologies for public outreach; empowering negotiators who can protect our interests while understanding those of our negotiating partners. There will be thousands of separate interactions, all strategically linked and coordinated to defend American security and prosperity. Diplomacy is hard work; but when we work hard, diplomacy can work, and not just to defuse tensions, but to achieve results that advance our security, interests, and values.

Secretary Gates has been particularly eloquent in articulating the importance of diplomacy in pursuit of our national security and foreign policy objectives. As he notes, it's not often that a secretary of defense makes the case for adding resources to the State Department and elevating the role of the diplomatic corps. Thankfully, Secretary Gates is more concerned about having a unified, agile, and effective U.S. strategy than in spending our precious time and energy on petty turf wars. As he has stated, "our civilian institutions of diplomacy and development have been chronically under-manned and underfunded for far too long," both relative to military spending and to "the responsibilities and challenges our nation has around the world." And to that, I say, "Amen!"

President-elect Obama has emphasized that the State Department must be fully empowered and funded to con-front multidimensional challenges—from working with allies to thwart terrorism, to spreading health and prosper-ity in places of human suffering. I will speak in greater detail about that in a moment.

We should also use the United Nations and other inter-national institutions whenever appropriate and possible. Both Democratic and Republican presidents have under-stood for decades that these institutions, when they work well, enhance our influence. And when they don't work well—as in the cases of Darfur and the farce of Sudan's election to the former UN Commission on Human Rights, for example—we should work with like-minded friends to make sure that these institutions reflect the values that motivated their creation in the first place.

We will lead with diplomacy because it's the smart approach. But we also know that military force will sometimes be necessary, and we will rely on it to protect our people and our interests when and where needed, as a last resort.

All the while, we must remember that to promote our interests around the world, America must be an exemplar of our values. Senator Isakson made the point to me the other day that our nation must lead by example rather than edict. Our history has shown that we are most effective when we see the harmony between our interests abroad and our values at home. And I take great comfort in knowing that our first secretary of state, Thomas Jefferson, also subscribed to that view, reminding us across the centuries: "The interests of a nation, when well understood, will be found to coincide with their moral duties."

So while our democracy continues to inspire people around the world, we know that its influence is greatest when we live up to its teachings ourselves.

Senator Lugar, I'm going to borrow your words here, because you have made this point so eloquently: You once said that "the United States cannot feed every person, lift every person out of poverty, cure every disease, or stop every conflict. But our power and status have conferred upon us a tremendous responsibility to humanity."

Of course, we must be realistic about achieving our goals. Even under the best of circumstances, our nation cannot solve every problem or meet every global need. We don't have unlimited time, treasure, or manpower. And we certainly don't face the best of circumstances today, with our economy faltering and our budget deficits growing.

So to fulfill our responsibility to our children, to protect and defend our nation while honoring our values, we have to establish priorities. Now, I'm not trying to mince words here. As my colleagues in the Senate know, "establishing priorities" means making tough choices. Because those choices are so important to the American people, we must be disciplined in evaluating them—weighing the costs and consequences of our action or inaction; gauging the probability of success; and insisting on measurable results.

Right after I was nominated, a friend told me: "The world has so many problems. You've got your work cut out for you." Well, I agree that the problems are many and they are big. But I don't get up every morning thinking only about the threats and dangers we face. With every challenge comes an opportunity to find promise and possibility in the face of adversity and complexity. Today's world calls forth the optimism and can-do spirit that has marked our progress for more than two centuries.

Too often we see the ills that plague us more clearly than the possibilities in front of us. We see threats that must be thwarted; wrongs that must be righted; conflicts that must be calmed. But not the partnerships that can be promoted; the rights that can be reinforced; the innovations that can be fostered; the people who can be empowered.

After all, it is the real possibility of progress—of that better life, free from fear and want and discord—that offers our most compelling message to the rest of the world.

I've had the chance to lay out and submit my views on a broad array of issues in written responses to questions from the committee, so in this statement I will outline some of the major challenges we face and some of the major opportunities we see.

First, President-elect Obama is committed to responsibly ending the war in Iraq and employing a broad strategy in Afghanistan that reduces threats to our safety and enhances the prospect of stability and peace.

Right now, our men and women in uniform, our diplomats, and our aid workers are risking their lives in those two countries. They have done everything we have asked of them and more. But, over time we have seen that our larger interests will be best served by safely and responsibly withdrawing our troops from Iraq, supporting a transition to full Iraqi responsibility for their sovereign nation, rebuilding our overtaxed military, and reaching out to other nations to help stabilize the region and to employ a broader arsenal of tools to fight terrorism.

Equally important will be a comprehensive plan using all elements of our power—diplomacy, development, and defense—to work with those in Afghanistan and Pakistan who want to root out al-Qaeda, the Taliban, and other violent extremists who threaten them as well as us in what

President-elect Obama has called the central front in the fight against terrorism. We need to deepen our engagement with these and other countries in the region and pursue policies that improve the lives of the Afghan and Pakistani people.

As we focus on Iraq, Pakistan, and Afghanistan, we must also actively pursue a strategy of smart power in the Middle East that addresses the security needs of Israel and the legitimate political and economic aspirations of the Palestinians; that effectively challenges Iran to end its nuclear weapons program and sponsorship of terror, and persuades both Iran and Syria to abandon their dangerous behavior and become constructive regional actors; that strengthens our relationships with Egypt, Jordan, Saudi Arabia, other Arab states, with Turkey, and with our partners in the Gulf to involve them in securing a lasting peace in the region.

As intractable as the Middle East's problems may seem—and many presidents, including my husband, have spent years trying to help work out a resolution—we cannot give up on peace. The president-elect and I understand and are deeply sympathetic to Israel's desire to defend itself under the current conditions, and to be free of shelling by Hamas rockets.

However, we have also been reminded of the tragic humanitarian costs of conflict in the Middle East, and pained by the suffering of Palestinian and Israeli civilians. This must only increase our determination to seek a just and lasting peace agreement that brings real security to Israel; normal and positive relations with its neighbors; and independence, economic progress, and security to the Palestinians in their own state. We will exert every effort to support the work of Israelis and Palestinians who seek that result. It is critical not only to the parties involved but to our profound interests in undermining the forces of alienation and violent extremism across our world.

Terrorism remains a serious threat, and we must have a comprehensive strategy, leveraging intelligence, diplomacy, and military assets to defeat al-Qaeda and like-minded terrorists by rooting out their networks and drying up support for their violent and nihilistic extremism. The gravest threat that America faces is the danger that weapons of mass destruction will fall into the hands of terrorists. To ensure our future security, we must curb the spread and use of these weapons—whether nuclear, biological, chemical, or cyber—while we take the lead in working with others to reduce current nuclear stockpiles and prevent the development and use of dangerous new weaponry.

Therefore, while defending against the threat of terrorism, we will also seize the parallel opportunity to get America back in the business of engaging other nations to reduce stockpiles of nuclear weapons. We will work with Russia to secure their agreement to extend essential monitoring and verification provisions of the START Treaty before it expires in December 2009, and we will work toward agreements for further reductions in nuclear weapons. We will also work with Russia to take U.S. and Russian missiles off hair-trigger alert, act with urgency to prevent proliferation in North Korea and Iran, secure loose nuclear weapons and materials, and shut down the market for selling them—as Senator Lugar has done for so many years.

The Non-Proliferation Treaty is the cornerstone of the nonproliferation regime, and the United States must exercise the leadership needed to shore up the regime. So, we will work with this committee and the Senate toward ratification of the Comprehensive Test Ban Treaty and reviving negotiations on a verifiable Fissile Material Cutoff Treaty.

Today's security threats cannot be addressed in isolation. Smart power requires reaching out to both friends and adversaries, to bolster old alliances and to forge new ones.

That means strengthening the alliances that have stood the test of time—especially with our NATO partners and our allies in Asia. Our alliance with Japan is a cornerstone of American policy in Asia, essential to maintaining peace and prosperity in the Asia-Pacific region, and based on shared values and mutual interests. We also have crucial economic and security partnerships with South Korea, Australia, and other friends in ASEAN. We will build on our economic and political partnership with India, the world's most populous democracy and a nation with growing influence in the world.

Our traditional relationships of confidence and trust with Europe will be deepened. Disagreements are inevitable, even among the closest friends, but on most global issues we have no more trusted allies. The new administration will have a chance to reach out across the Atlantic to leaders in France, Germany, the United Kingdom, and others across the continent, including the new democracies. When America and Europe work together, global objectives are well within our means.

President-elect Obama and I seek a future of cooperative engagement with the Russian government on matters of strategic importance, while standing up strongly for American values and international norms.

China is a critically important actor in a changing global landscape. We want a positive and cooperative relationship with China, one where we deepen and strengthen our ties on a number of issues, and candidly address differences where they persist.

But this not a one-way effort—much of what we will do depends on the choices China makes about its future at home and abroad.

With both Russia and China, we should work together on vital security and economic issues like terrorism, proliferation, climate change, and reforming financial markets.

The world is now in the cross currents of the most severe global economic contraction since the Great Depression. The history of that crisis teaches us the consequences of diplomatic failures and uncoordinated reactions. Yet history alone is an insufficient guide; the world has changed too much. We have already seen that this crisis extends beyond the housing and banking sectors, and our solutions will have to be as wide in scope as the causes themselves, taking into account the complexities of the global economy, the geopolitics involved, and the likelihood of continued political and economic repercussions from the damage already done.

But here again, as we work to repair the damage, we can find new ways of working together. For too long, we have merely talked about the need to engage emerging powers in global economic governance; the time to take action is upon us. The recent G-20 meeting was a first step, but developing patterns of sustained engagement will take hard work and careful negotiation. We know that emerging markets like China, India, Brazil, South Africa, and Indonesia are feeling the effects of the current crisis. We all stand to benefit in both the short and long term if they are part of the solution, and become partners in maintaining global economic stability. In our efforts to return to economic growth here in the United States, we have an especially critical need to work more closely with Canada, our largest trading partner, and Mexico, our third largest. Canada and Mexico are also our biggest suppliers of imported energy. More broadly, we must build a deeper partnership with Mexico to address the shared danger arising from drug trafficking and the challenges of our border, an effort begun this week with a meeting between President-elect Obama and President Calderon.

Throughout our hemisphere we have opportunities to enhance cooperation to meet common economic, security, and environmental objectives that affect us all. We will return to a policy of vigorous engagement throughout Latin America, seeking deeper understanding and broader engagement with nations from the Caribbean to Central to South America. Not only do we share common political, economic, and strategic interests with our friends to the south, our relationship is also enhanced by many shared ancestral and cultural legacies. We are looking forward to working on many issues during the Summit of the Americas in April and taking up the president-elect's call for a new energy partnership of the Americas built around shared technology and new investments in renewable energy.

In Africa, the foreign policy objectives of the Obama administration are rooted in security, political, economic, and humanitarian interests, including combating al-Qaeda's efforts to seek safe havens in failed states in the Horn of Africa; helping African nations to conserve their natural resources and reap fair benefits from them; stopping war in Congo; ending autocracy in Zimbabwe and human devastation in Darfur; supporting African democracies like South Africa and Ghana (which just had its second change of power in democratic elections); and working aggres-